THE GREAT LIVES SERIES

Great Lives biographies shed an exciting new light on the many dynamic men and women whose actions, visions, and dedication to an ideal have influenced the course of history. Their ambitions, dreams, successes, and failures, the controversies they faced and the obstacles they overcame are the true stories behind these distinguished world leaders, explorers, and great Americans.

Other biographies in the Great Lives Series

GREAT LIVES

JESSE JACKSON
A VOICE FOR CHANGE

By Steven Otfinoski

FAWCETT COLUMBINE
NEW YORK

For middle-school readers

A Fawcett Columbine Book
Published by Ballantine Books

Produced by
The Jeffrey Weiss Group, Inc.
96 Morton Street
New York, New York 10014

Library of Congress Catalog Card Number: 89-90905

ISBN:0-449-90402-4

Cover design and illustration by Paul Davis

Manufactured in the United States of America

First Edition: February 1990

10 9 8 7 6 5 4

ACKNOWLEDGMENT

A special thanks to educators Dr. Frank Moretti, Ph.D., Associate Headmaster of the Dalton School in New York City; Dr. Paul Mattingly, Ph.D., Professor of History at New York University; and Barbara Smith, M.S., Assistant Superintendent of the Los Angeles Unified School District, for their contributions to the Great Lives Series.

JESSE JACKSON
A VOICE FOR CHANGE

TABLE OF CONTENTS

1

Keeping Hope Alive

I T WAS ANOTHER hot, sticky summer night in
Atlanta, Georgia. But the heat was not the main
thing on the minds of the several thousand people
at the 1988 Democratic National Convention in the
Omni Coliseum. They were waiting anxiously to hear
the man who had dominated the Democratic race for
president and had captured the imagination of millions of Americans. Everyone knew by now that this
man would not be their candidate for president, but
whether he would enthusiastically support the winning ticket was a matter of great concern. The man
they were waiting for was Jesse Louis Jackson.

Jackson was not just another runner-up for the
nomination. In a field of seven candidates, he was one
of only two to survive the long, grueling round of state
primaries. The seven million votes he had earned had
not been enough to win the nomination. That prize
was about to go to his chief rival, Massachusetts Gov-

ernor Michael Dukakis. There had been high hopes that Dukakis would choose Jesse as his running mate, but he was passed over for vice president, too. Jesse had been disappointed by the way he felt Dukakis's campaign team had ignored him and his supporters. There had been a peace meeting between the two men the previous day, but there were still doubts in many people's minds about how strongly Jackson would support Dukakis and his running mate, Senator Lloyd Bentsen of Texas. In another few minutes, the crowd in the Omni Coliseum, and the rest of America watching the convention on television, would know where Jesse Jackson stood.

The first Jackson to step out on the speaker's rostrum, however, was neither the candidate nor his wife, but their five children. They spoke passionately about their father and his achievements. After a brief film about the candidate was shown, Jesse Jr., Jackson's eldest son, introduced "a man who fights against the odds, who lives against the odds, our dad, Jesse Jackson."

Thunderous applause and cheering erupted throughout the hall as the six-foot-two, 200-pound candidate strode up to the rostrum. With his neat moustache, dark, piercing eyes, and strikingly handsome features, the 46-year-old Jackson looked as much a movie star as a presidential candidate. Chants of "Jesse! Jesse! Jesse!" filled the air. As the band played "America the Beautiful" and then "The Stars and Stripes Forever," the tall black man mounted the podium and pumped his fist three times for victory.

Minutes passed before the crowd quieted down. Then Jesse Jackson did a gracious thing. Instead of launching into his speech, he introduced a frail, elderly black woman seated in the stands. She was Rosa Parks, and Jackson called her "the mother of the Civil-Rights Movement." Some thirty years earlier, Rosa Parks had earned that title when she took a seat in the front of a segregated city bus in Montgomery, Alabama, and refused to move when the bus driver ordered her to give up her seat to a white person. She was arrested for breaking a local law that required blacks to sit in the back of public buses. Her arrest led to a yearlong boycott of Montgomery buses led by the then unknown Martin Luther King, Jr. King went on to become the leader of America's Civil-Rights Movement. He was assassinated in 1968.

Mrs. Parks stood and acknowledged the crowd's ovation. After she sat down again, Jesse began to speak to the delegates in loud, ringing words. "Dr. Martin Luther King, Jr., lies only a few miles from us tonight," he began. "Tonight he must feel good as he looks down upon us. We sit here together, a rainbow coalition — the sons and daughters of slave-masters, and the sons and daughters of slaves — sitting together around a common table, to decide the direction of our party and our country.

"Common ground!" he exclaimed. "That's the challenge of our party tonight." Jackson spoke of unity not just within the Democratic party, but among all Americans, regardless of creed and color. Then he saluted Dukakis, the man who had beat him for the nomination. "His foreparents came to America on immigrant ships. My foreparents came to America on slave ships. But whatever the original ships, we are in the same boat tonight.

"America is not a blanket woven from one thread, one color, one cloth," he told his audience. He spoke of his childhood in Greenville, South Carolina, and how his grandmother made a patchwork quilt to keep him warm, because she couldn't afford a blanket.

"With sturdy hands and a strong cord, she sewed them together into a quilt, a thing of beauty and power and culture," he explained. "Now, Democrats, we must build such a quilt."

One by one, he addressed the special interest groups of America — farmers, workers, women, students, blacks, Hispanics, conservatives, and liberals. He told each of them that "your patch is not big enough . . . your point of view is not enough. But don't despair. Be as wise as my grandma. Pull the patches and pieces together, bound by a common thread. When we form a great quilt of unity and common ground . . . we the people can win."

Jackson's speech, full of power and conviction, lasted for fifty-one minutes. When he drew toward the end he looked directly into the television cameras and addressed one constituency in particular. It was the one he had fought for and served long before he ever thought of running for president — the poor.

"Wherever you are tonight, you can make it," he told them. "Hold your head high. Stick your chest out. You can make it. It gets dark sometimes, but the morning comes. Don't you surrender. Suffering breeds character, character breeds faith. In the end, faith will not disappoint. . . . Keep hope alive!"

Jesse then left the podium and made his way through a sea of people. The convention hall resounded with cheers and applause. Those who weren't cheering or yelling were crying, for Jackson had moved them deeply with a speech that many were already calling one of the greatest in American political history. Former President Jimmy Carter later told a reporter that it was the best speech ever given at a convention, "certainly in my lifetime." Grown men were seen choking back tears. One white delegate from Mississippi had his arms around his black friend, the state delegate chairman. "When a man like Jesse speaks out for you," he said, wiping tears from his eyes, "you really believe you can achieve something."

Jesse knew of what he spoke. Everyone *could* achieve something, *be* somebody, no matter who they were. Jackson believed it, because he had lived it. The speech had been an eloquent summing up of not just his beliefs, but of his entire life. The journey he had made from a rickety house in Greenville, South Carolina, to the Omni Coliseum in Atlanta, Georgia, had been a long and difficult one. But for Jesse Jackson it had been a worthy struggle, one that had shaped him into a man who could aspire to be president of the United States.

2

Growing Up in Greenville

TWO THINGS DISTINGUISHED the sleepy Southern town of Greenville, South Carolina, in the 1940s. First, its many fabric-producing textile mills made it the "textile capital of the world." Second, like many other Southern towns and cities, it was strictly segregated between blacks and whites.

Slavery had ended in the United States in the 1860s. In 1863, President Abraham Lincoln issued the Emancipation Proclamation, which outlawed the practice and declared the slaves to be free. But black people, although free, remained second-class citizens with few rights. They lived in the poorest neighborhoods of towns. They had the lowest-paying jobs. They weren't allowed in restaurants, movie houses, and hotels frequented by white people. They weren't even allowed to drink from the same water fountains. Their children received an inferior education at all-black schools. This is the way things were in much of the southern United States in 1940. This is the way they would remain for the next twenty-five years.

In 1941 two historic events occurred in Greenville, South Carolina. The Ku Klux Klan, an all-white racist organization, marched through the town of 60,000. Its members, dressed in white robes and hoods that hid their identity, hated blacks and tried to terrify them through tactics such as lynchings, arson, and general harassment. The intolerance they symbolized would live on for a long time.

That same year, Greenville's most famous citizen was born in a humble house on Ridge Street in a poor but respectable black neighborhood. His name was Jesse Jackson, and he would grow up to fight and triumph over the racism and injustice the Klan stood for.

The circumstances surrounding Jesse's birth were anything but special. Helen Burns, his mother, was eighteen years old at the time and a junior in high school. Helen was a bright girl who attended the Springfield Baptist Church. She had a beautiful voice, sang spirituals in church, and played lead roles in school operettas. She was also one of the few people in her neighborhood who could read and write, and earned the gratitude of her illiterate neighbors by filling out their Social Security forms for them.

Helen's next-door neighbor was an older man named Noah Louis Robinson. Noah was a cotton grader by trade, but also served as a deacon in the Baptist Church. He was a handsome, distinguished-looking man, highly respected in the community. It was not surprising that Helen Burns fell in love with him. However, the neighborhood was scandalized when it was learned that Helen was pregnant with Noah Robinson's child, for Noah was married to another woman. Helen had to drop out of high school and was forced to leave the church where she had been a lifelong member.

On October 8, 1941, Helen gave birth at home to a healthy, seven-pound four-ounce baby boy. The midwife who helped her remembered the birth vividly. "It seemed that the child was in a hurry to get there," she recalled later. "By the time the doctor arrived, I had just wrapped him in a blanket and laid him in bed with his mother."

Helen named the child Jesse, after Noah's father, the Reverend Jesse Robinson, founder of the Mount Emmanuel Baptist Church in Greenville. Four of Jesse Robinson's brothers were also preachers. The newborn Jesse had a rich ethnic heritage as well. On his father's side, he was the descendant of Cherokee Indians. On his mother's side, he was the descendant of slaves and an Irish plantation owner.

Noah Robinson was not ashamed of Helen or their son. In fact he was extremely proud, and told anyone who would listen that his son was his "spitting image."

Helen continued to live on Ridge Street. Everyone was elated when she married Charles Henry Jackson, when Jesse was two years old. Jackson was an excellent athlete who had dreams of becoming a professional baseball player. However, at twenty-four he gave up that dream and took a job in the post office to support his new family. Charles Jackson was a good stepfather to Jesse and officially adopted him when the boy was sixteen.

Still, none of this changed the fact that Jesse Jackson was born out of wedlock. The other children taunted and teased him about it on the street and in the playground. "You're a nothing and a nobody," they jeered. Jesse never forgot those words. In his heart he vowed he would prove them wrong. One day he would be somebody, he swore to himself. He would be somebody that people listened to and respected, just like his real father, Noah Robinson.

Two positive forces in Jesse's childhood were to have a powerful influence on his future. One was the Baptist Church. Religion and the church were the heart and soul of the black community in the South. They provided inspiration and comfort for a people who faced injustice every day of their lives. Almost from the time he could walk, Jesse made the three-mile trip every Sunday to the Longbranch Baptist Church with his family. When he was four, he got his first role in a church play. The boy had a natural gift for speaking in front of people that did not go unnoticed.

"Jesse was an unusual kind of fella, even when he was just learning to talk," recalled his father, Noah Robinson. "He would say he was going to be a preacher. He would say, 'I'm going to lead people through the rivers of water.'"

Jesse gave his first public speech in church during a Christmas pageant. People were so impressed by his ability to communicate that at age nine he was sent to a National Sunday School Convention in

Charlotte, North Carolina, to represent his church. Soon he was giving an oral report to the congregation every month.

The other major influence in young Jesse's life was his favorite relative, his grandmother Matilda Burns, who he called "Aunt Tibby." Tibby had never gone to school, but she was a wise and thoughtful person. In her wisdom she recognized the great potential in her grandson.

Aunt Tibby worked in the homes of middle-class white families in Greenville. When her employers were through reading their copies of *National Geographic* and other magazines and books, Tibby would bring them home for Jesse to read. She encouraged him to read and learn all he could in school. She also told him to avoid violence and always be clean because "cleanliness is next to Godliness." Most important of all, she built up his self-confidence. "When God made you, he did his best work," she told Jesse. "If you've got the guts, there isn't anything you can't do."

Jesse believed those words, and set out to be somebody. He landed his first job at age six. His grandfather, who owned a lumberyard, needed a helper. The two would drive into the countryside in a pickup truck, find slabs of wood, saw them into firewood for stoves, and bring them back to sell in town. As Jesse grew older, he found many other jobs. At local football games he sold food and souvenirs — the first black boy in Greenville's history to do so. He shined shoes in his stepfather's shoe-shine parlor. He sold tickets at the local Liberty Movie Theatre. He waited

11

on tables at a local restaurant. He even became a golf caddy at the Greenville Country Club.

To Jesse, the white people he met at the country club seemed as if they were from another world. They wore fine clothes, always had plenty of money, appeared to have no worries, and generally looked to be very successful in life. Jesse wanted to be like them. He spent some of the money he earned buying the used clothing of the country-club set in second-hand stores. His friends teased him and said he was "putting on airs." Jesse paid them no heed; he was determined to make something of himself.

However, for a black person of any age to be somebody in the South in the 1950s was difficult. Segregation and racial injustice were the grim facts of life. In fact, when he was only six, Jesse had a shocking experience with racial prejudice that he would never forget.

A favorite hangout for Jesse and his friends was a corner grocery store run by a white man named Jack. Jack got along well with the black youths, and Jesse considered him a friend. One day Jesse entered the store at a particularly busy time to buy some candy. To get Jack's attention from the other customers, he whistled loudly. The "friendly" store owner pulled a gun out from behind the counter and aimed it directly at the shocked young boy. "Don't ever whistle at a white man as long as you live," said Jack threateningly. No one in the crowded store said a word in Jesse's defense or tried to take away the gun. Jesse walked out shaking with fear. There was no doubt in his mind that the gun pointed at him had been loaded. He learned an important lesson that day — that the roots of prejudice and fear ran far deeper than he had ever suspected.

His experiences at school also made Jesse painfully aware that he was living in a racist society. Though there was an elementary school only two blocks from Jesse's home, Jesse was not permitted to attend because it was for white students only. Instead, he had to walk five miles each day to the all-black Nicholtown School.

The adult Jesse once described Nicholtown as a rather grim place: "There was no grass in the yard. I couldn't play, couldn't roll over because our school yard was full of sand. And if it rained, it turned into red dirt."

Inside, the school was no better. The few textbooks — hand-me-downs from the white school — were old and falling apart. Sometimes as many as five or six students had to share one book. Homework often went unassigned because no one person could take books home.

Despite these drawbacks, Jesse Jackson was determined to learn. In the sixth grade he joined a reading club at the County Library for the Colored. He worked hard at his studies and just as hard on the playing field. A big, gangling boy at twelve, Jesse's dream was to become a football star.

That dream began to come true when Jesse entered the all-black Sterling High School in 1955. He went out for and made the football, basketball, and baseball teams. "He was a fierce competitor," recalled his football coach Rev. D.J. Mathis. "He played every game to win." Mathis said Jesse was the best quarterback he ever coached. Jesse proved his coach's faith in him by making the state championship team.

Yet for all his intense interest in sports, Jesse never let academics suffer. If he missed a class because of a practice or game, he always made up the assignment — the only athlete at Sterling High to do so. He was as popular with his fellow students as he was with his teachers. He was elected president of his freshman class, as well as president of the student council and honor society. If there was an office to run for, Jesse ran, and usually won.

Some of his teachers found Jesse's drive and ambition a little overwhelming. "I always teased him that he's first person singular, not plural," said Xanthen Norris, his high school French teacher. "Always an 'I' person. I *am* somebody. That's something that's always been with Jesse."

His natural ability at public speaking and his sharp sense of humor made him a hit at lunchtime. "He was like Richard Pryor, Bill Cosby, and Redd Foxx combined," recalled his half brother Noah Robinson, Jr. "He had the whole place cracking up." In fact, most of his classmates predicted that if Jesse didn't make it as a pro athlete, he'd become a successful comedian.

But something besides schoolwork and sports was becoming the focus of Jesse's attention at this time in his life. A new black minister had come to Greenville. His name was Reverend James Hall and he was different from all the other preachers Jesse had ever heard. Jesse was accustomed to hearing sermons about heaven and the rewards that awaited black people in the next life. Reverend Hall was more interested in *this* life and how blacks could improve their lives here and now by standing up for their rights. Jesse was impressed by Reverend Hall and his message. He had grown up wondering why things were the way they were. Here was a man saying to him that they didn't have to be that way at all.

An incident soon took place that gave Reverend Hall a chance to put his preaching into practice. Jackie Robinson, the first black athlete to play professional baseball, was stopping over at the Greenville Airport. A famous celebrity and ballplayer, Robinson decided to have a meal while waiting for his flight out, but airport officials refused to allow him to be served in the airport restaurant. Reverend Hall and other black people in Greenville were enraged, and held a protest march against Robinson's shabby treatment. In a passionate speech, Hall called for all blacks to speak out for their rights and to reject segregation. In the mid-1950s, this was a bold and brave thing to do.

Young Jesse Jackson got the message. One of his after-school jobs was cleaning machines at a local bakery. Jesse and his friend, Owen Perkins, attempted to organize the bakery's black workers to protest the fact that black workers were segregated from white workers and received less pay. The protest failed, but Jesse realized that organized, peaceful protest could bring about change, if enough people were behind it.

15

As graduation grew near, Jesse's dream of being a pro-football player remained strong. Game after game, he proved himself a winning quarterback. But few people outside of the black community knew or cared about Jesse's athletic triumphs. The sad fact was that the local newspapers gave little coverage to black athletes at Sterling High. All the headlines and glory went to the white athletes at Greenville High, especially top quarterback Dickie Dietz. On one occasion, Greenville won a game 7-6. That same day Jesse scored three touchdowns to lead his team to victory, 20-6. The local paper's top headline on the sports page read, "Dietz Kicks Extra Point. Greenville Wins." Jesse's much greater achievement was tucked away in a small article at the bottom of the page.

Jesse hoped things would be more equal in the bigger world of pro sports. After graduating in 1959, he went to a pro-baseball tryout camp for the summer. He was the only black player there. Jesse thought he might follow in the footsteps of his stepfather and pursue a career in baseball. He was offered a job playing with the Chicago White Sox, but before he could decide whether to take the offer, professional football's New York Giants made him a better one — a starting salary of $6,000 a year. There was no doubt in Jesse's mind which offer he'd take. Football was still his first love.

Then the young black man got a shock. Dickie Dietz, his main rival in Greenville, was also offered a spot with the Giants. But Dietz's salary was going to be $95,000 a year — over fifteen times what was offered to Jesse! Jesse knew Dietz hadn't been offered more money because he was a better player than Jesse. Rather, it was because he was white and Jesse was black. Once again racism was holding him down, keeping him from fulfilling his full potential. This time he was determined to do something about it.

Jesse turned down the Giants' offer and instead accepted a football scholarship to the University of Illinois in Chicago. This way he would be able to play football and at the same time get a good education. Jesse knew his chances of success were much better if he had a college degree.

Jesse expected to find less prejudice in the North, and more opportunity for black people. Once again, he would be sorely disappointed.

3

Football, Romance, and Civil Rights

JESSE JACKSON'S FIRST rude awakening about racism in the North came when he reported to football practice at the University of Illinois in the fall of 1959. When he expressed his desire to play quarterback, the position at which he had excelled in high school, his coach just shook his head.

"There are no black quarterbacks on this team," he said. "Black players are linemen, regardless of how well they play."

Bitterly, Jesse realized that once again he was a black man in a white world, and that he had to play by that world's rules. It didn't matter where he went, the rules stayed the same.

Sports was only one aspect of the problem, Jesse quickly learned. Although classes at the university were integrated, once the bell rang, black and white students went their separate ways. Black students were excluded from many school activities and couldn't join fraternities or sororities. On weekends, Jesse once recalled, black students "sat in their dorm drinking Coke and playing cards," while many white students were having a good time at parties and dances.

Jesse returned home during Christmas vacation disappointed and unhappy. It was good to be back among his family and friends. But when he went down to the local library to work on his school assignments, he wasn't allowed in. Nothing had changed in Greenville. He may have been a student at a prominent university, but in his hometown he was still a black man. Since it was too noisy and crowded at home to study, Jesse was forced to return to school early in order to complete his work.

Back in Chicago, Jesse was more frustrated than ever. Then, one night in February 1960, he was watching the news on television and saw something remarkable. Four black students were shown sitting at a lunch counter at a Woolworth's store in Greensboro, North Carolina. The waitress had refused to serve them when they ordered coffee, but instead of turning and leaving, the students had refused to move until they were served. A tense standoff ensued. Finally, the police arrived on the scene and carried the four off to jail.

This was the first time Jesse had ever seen a sit-in protesting segregation in the South. This was the kind of civil disobedience that Reverend Hall had preached about back home in Greenville. Here were students, just like Jesse, refusing to be treated like second-class citizens. They had brought their protest to the attention of the entire nation on television! When Jesse learned that the four students attended the all-black North Carolina Agricultural and Technical State College in Greensboro, he decided that was the school for him. After completing one year at the University of Illinois, Jesse applied to and was accepted as a first-year student at A. & T.

At his new school, Jesse Jackson positively blossomed. He made the football team and became the star quarterback. He was elected student-body president and was an honor student and an officer of the Omega Psi Phi fraternity. Most important of all, he became deeply involved in the growing Civil-Rights Movement. He joined the newly formed Congress of Racial Equality (CORE), a national civil-rights organization, and for nearly a year organized and led sit-ins and demonstrations almost daily. The goal of the demonstrations was to integrate downtown Greensboro. It was a major challenge that Jesse took on with gusto and energy. He led student demonstrations at local restaurants, hotels, and movie houses that refused to admit blacks.

In 1963, during a march in front of the Greensboro Town Hall, Jesse was arrested by police. "I'm going to jail," he told his supporters. "And I'll go to the chain gang if necessary. All I want is freedom for my people." The awful conditions he saw in the Greensboro jail gave Jesse another cause to fight for. He promised jail conditions would change, too.

21

Despite his constant work for civil rights, Jesse still found time to relax and have fun like any other college student. A handsome young man, he was popular with the girls on campus and never lacked a date. In his sophomore year, however, he met one girl who made him forget all the others. Her name was Jacqueline Lavinia Brown, a pretty freshman from Virginia.

One day, Jesse was standing outside the student hall chatting with some friends, when Jackie walked by. "Hey, baby, I'm going to marry you!" shouted Jesse. Jackie was so startled she walked straight into a mud puddle and ruined a new pair of shoes. "That put us on bad terms to start with," she remembered, "although he said he was sorry and offered to help me. But when we met later in a class we had together, I found him to be very bright and sensitive."

It wasn't long before Jackie was going to church every Sunday with Jesse and standing by his side at protest marches. The young couple was married in 1962, in Jesse's parents' living room in Greenville. "It was a lovely little country wedding," recalled Jackie. Her younger brothers and sisters didn't make the trip from Virginia, but listened to the ceremony on the telephone.

By this time, Jesse Jackson was truly becoming "somebody." The sit-ins and protest marches were working: Greensboro was gradually becoming integrated. Indeed, Jesse's leadership made him something of a celebrity throughout the state of North Carolina.

While he was gaining experience in the street,

Jesse was also studying black civil rights and history in the classroom. One of his professors, Dr. Leonard Robinson, introduced him to the great black leaders of the past. One of them was Frederick Douglass, a leader in the fight against slavery. Another was W. E. B. Du Bois, who campaigned for black equality early in the twentieth century. But it was contemporary leaders that Jesse was most drawn to. He admired Malcolm X, a black minister and religious leader, and Dr. Martin Luther King, Jr., head of the Southern Christian Leadership Conference (SCLC). King's philosophy of nonviolent civil disobedience attracted Jesse, and Dr. King became his role model and hero.

In 1964, Jesse graduated from North Carolina A. & T. with a B. A. degree in sociology. He worked briefly for North Carolina governor Terry Sanford, organizing young Democrats, but politics wasn't fulfilling enough for him. Dr. King and most of the black leaders he admired were ministers, men of God. While still in college, Jesse had thought seriously about joining their ranks. His college roommate recalled how one night Jesse woke him up to tell him about a strange dream he had had. "He said that he thought he had been called to preach," said the roommate. "He was shaking. I never saw him look so serious before."

Jesse was serious. In 1965, he accepted a grant from the Rockefeller Foundation to study at the Chicago Theological Seminary. With his wife and new daughter, Santita, Jesse moved back to the city which had rejected him six years before.

Chicago had changed little in that time. It was the

nation's third largest city, with one of the biggest and poorest black ghettos in the United States. Looking at the poverty and misery around him, Jesse immediately felt torn between the call of the religious life and the call of social action. At first, he tried to heed both. He studied hard in seminary school and got involved in civil-rights work. He joined the League of Chicago Neighborhood Groups and, more importantly, Dr. King's SCLC. In the black neighborhoods of Chicago's South Side, Jesse tried to organize people to protest against poor housing, low pay, and over-priced goods from local stores mostly owned by white people. But he found stiff resistance. Many people were afraid to get involved. Even black ministers, leaders in the black community, didn't want to protest out of fear of losing church funds from the city.

This was frustrating for Jackson, especially when he saw the progress Martin Luther King, Jr., was making in the South. There, major battles for civil rights were being fought daily. When King announced that he would march from Selma to Montgomery, Alabama, to protest the denial of black voting rights, Jesse decided to join the march. He organized half of the students from the seminary to make the long drive south to Alabama. It was to be a historic occasion for the Civil-Rights Movement, and for Jesse Jackson as well.

In Selma, Jesse met his hero face-to-face for the first time. "King was like a giant," he later recalled. "He was not afraid of violence and bullets and bombs." Dr. King's first impression of the young graduate student was mixed. He admired Jesse's organizational abilities and his earnestness. But it bothered him when Jesse sometimes appeared too ambitious. King felt that Jackson spoke out as if he were an SCLC staff member when he was just another protesting student.

Atlanta Mayor Andrew Young, who was then an aide to Dr. King, once said that Jesse was "merely a face in the crowd in Selma." Young himself remembers being annoyed when Jesse stepped out of the crowd and started ordering marchers around. A reporter on the scene later recalled that at first, when Jackson delivered a passionate speech, she wondered who he was. "He just seemed to have come from nowhere," she said. "But he spoke so well, I recorded his statement anyway. I had the feeling that one day he might be important."

In early 1966, Dr. King and his staff came to Chicago to start the Chicago Freedom Movement. Their goal was to free Chicago's blacks from poverty and injustice. King remembered the eager young student from Selma and welcomed Jesse's help in organizing students for sit-ins and demonstrations.

Chicago proved to be as tough a town to integrate as any city in the South. Some white residents didn't take kindly to black outsiders marching in their neighborhoods. On one occasion Jesse was struck in the head by a brick thrown during a march. Even Dr. King was injured once.

But the violence only deepened Jesse's commitment to social change. Ralph Abernathy, King's top lieutenant, was impressed by Jesse and persuaded King to consider making room for the young man on the SCLC staff. Jesse knew he couldn't afford to miss such a golden opportunity. His dream of being a pro athlete had long given way to a much greater dream. He now wanted to be somebody who could help other people, many of them black like him, to become somebodies, too.

He still wanted to be a preacher, but he soon realized that the whole city of Chicago could be his pulpit. One semester away from graduation, Jesse Jackson left the seminary to work full-time for Martin Luther King, Jr. At twenty-four, he became the youngest member of the SCLC staff. It was a decision that would change his life and that of millions of Americans.

4

Working for the King

MARTIN LUTHER KING, Jr., found stiff opposition to his efforts to improve the housing and employment situation of Chicago's blacks. That opposition centered on one person — Chicago Mayor Richard J. Daley. Daley was a masterful politician who had run the city with a strong hand since 1955. He resented Dr. King coming to his city and telling him how to change things, and tried to stop King's protest marches. When this failed, Daley made an agreement with King: He would help end housing discrimination against blacks if the civil-rights leader would stop marching. King held up his end of the bargain, but Daley didn't. Racial discrimination continued as it had before. King left Chicago defeated and discouraged.

However, he left behind a man who he hoped would carry on the fight for a better life for Chicago's poor. That man was Jesse Jackson. King had watched Jesse grow and mature under his influence, and he had come to feel that the young man was ready for a responsible position in his organization. He put Jackson in charge of the Chicago branch of the SCLC's Operation Breadbasket.

The goal of Operation Breadbasket, which King had started in Atlanta in 1962, was to bring food and money to the urban poor. While marches and sit-ins had been effective weapons in the overtly racist South, Jesse had learned from Dr. King's experiences in Chicago that these would not work as well in the North. Discrimination was more subtle in the North, and politicians, such as Mayor Daley, were more sophisticated. Thus, a different approach was needed to triumph over racism. Economic boycotts were the method of choice.

A boycott occurs when a group of people refuses to patronize a particular store or business in order to change the way it operates. In Chicago's South Side there were plenty of businesses that needed changing. Many stores in the black ghettos were owned by white people who overcharged black customers and refused to hire them. These businesses took millions of dollars from the ghetto and gave nothing back in return. Jesse decided that boycotts would be the most effective way to force these stores to change their practices. "We are the margin of profit of every major item produced in America," Jesse told the black community, "from General Motors on down to Kellogg's Corn Flakes."

To begin, Jesse was in no position to take on General Motors. His operation was a decidedly modest one.

His first headquarters was his crowded apartment on the city's South Side, where he lived with Jackie and their now three children. The youngest, Jonathan Luther, was named after Jesse's boss and hero, Martin Luther King, Jr.

Operation Breadbasket's first target was a local dairy-store chain called Country Delight. The company owned 104 stores in black neighborhoods but employed no black milk-truck drivers or salespersons. Jesse asked them to change their hiring policies. When they refused, he called for a boycott of all Country Delight stores. The message was carried into the black community by one hundred black ministers from their church pulpits.

The boycott was effective and brief. Country Delight's managers watched their unsold milk turn sour and other products go bad. After just three days, they gave in and agreed to hire forty-four blacks.

Fresh from this first victory, Jesse went after other businesses. Some, who wanted to avoid a boycott and negative publicity, agreed to Operation Breadbasket's demands without putting up a fight. "They heard our footsteps coming," is how Jesse put it. In only five months, nine Chicago companies agreed to hire more blacks and provide those already working for them with better pay and benefits.

The manager of one supermarket chain that refused to give in called Jesse a liar and an opportunist. "Yes, I am an opportunist for justice," Jesse readily admitted, "because I seize every opportunity to try to right a wrong, whether it's in schools, stores, or anywhere black people are being disrespected." A short time later, Jesse's boycott forced the chain out of business.

Jesse's biggest challenge was a much larger supermarket chain — A & P, one of Chicago's oldest and most respected supermarkets. A & P had forty stores on the South Side, but not one black person held a manager's position. When Jesse called for a boycott, A & P decided to tough it out. The company figured that its vast resources would enable it to survive a boycott without yielding to black people's demands. But after four months and a loss of $10 million in sales, the mighty chain was ready to meet at the negotiating table. They agreed to hire black managers for their supermarkets, as well as hundreds of other blacks to fill different jobs. They also agreed to stock twenty-five products made by black businesses, including orange juice, bread, and a milk named after the great black heavyweight boxer, Joe Louis. Jesse pointed out to his supporters that Joe Louis Milk didn't come from a "Negro cow" and had the same nutrients as any other milk. "[The] only difference is that your husband can make twelve thousand dollars a year driving a truck for this company," he explained.

The successful boycott of A & P was a stunning victory for Operation Breadbasket. For one thing, the black people of Chicago realized the power they wielded with their pocketbooks — so did the white establishment. In addition, Jesse Jackson so impressed Dr. King with his leadership abilities that after only a year King appointed him the national director of Operation Breadbasket. Jesse opened up

Jesse with his mentor, Martin Luther King, Jr., the famed civil-rights leader, on the balcony of the Memphis motel where King was assassinated on April 4, 1968, the day after this photo was taken. Although the two passionate activists didn't always agree on tactics, they both fought toward the same goal, and Jackson has come to be acknowledged as King's true successor.

branches of the organization in twenty cities across the country, including New York, Houston, and Los Angeles. While these new branches did some good, they were less effective than the Chicago operation. This was because they lacked the grass-roots support that Jesse had so carefully built up in what had become his home city.

Meanwhile, Jesse was broadening his base of power in Chicago. He knew that communication was the key to bringing people together to solve their problems. He began holding meetings every Saturday morning at the Chicago Theological Seminary, where he was once a student. The meetings were small at first, including mostly leaders in the black community. But as word got out, more and more people started coming. Soon the attendance swelled from hundreds to thousands, forcing a move to the Capitol Theatre in downtown Chicago. The highlight of each meeting was Jesse's passionate and eloquent speech, which sounded more like a sermon.

Jesse was a unique orator. He combined the idealism of a fiery preacher with the practical thinking of a committed politician. He spoke about important issues and complex ideas, but always on a level that the simplest person could understand. He knew the power of a brief, well-worded slogan, and his speeches were studded with them.

"I am somebody!" he shouted out from his pulpit in the Capital Theater. "I am somebody!" the crowd roared back in response. "I am black, beautiful, and proud!" he told them. He was a speaker who could express the hopes and needs of people and rouse them to action that would fulfill those dreams. Indeed, many felt that in this respect he was second only to Martin Luther King, Jr., himself.

"Everybody went," remembered one woman about the meetings. "Some Saturdays the place was so jammed you'd have to get there early or you didn't get a seat." Those who couldn't get a seat at the Capital could listen to Jesse's sermon on the radio. He was rapidly becoming one of the most outspoken and best-known voices in Chicago.

Jackson's and King's actions were having the desired effect. People's attitudes were changing, and so were laws. President John F. Kennedy, elected in 1960, supported the Civil-Rights Movement. So did his successor, Lyndon B. Johnson, who took office after Kennedy's assassination in 1963 and was elected president in 1964. Johnson helped end racial discrimination with his forceful support of a series of new laws.

The Civil Rights Act of 1964 outlawed discrimination in restaurants, hotels, and the workplace. The Voting Rights Act of 1965 barred the unfair use of literacy tests in a number of Southern states to prevent blacks from becoming registered voters. In 1966 the Supreme Court put an end to poll taxes, which had prevented blacks from voting in state and local elections. Indeed, black Americans were on the threshold of their greatest achievements since President Abraham Lincoln had freed them from slavery in 1863. But just when the Promised Land seemed within reach, the Civil-Rights Movement lost its greatest leader.

33

In February 1968, 1,300 sanitation workers — both black and white — in Memphis, Tennessee, went on strike for better pay and working conditions. By early April, the action had seen violent confrontations with the police in which one person had died and 238 others had been arrested. Martin Luther King, Jr., looking to broaden his base and show that he could help working people whatever the color of their skin, decided to go to Memphis to support the strikers. He also wanted to put an end to the violence.

On April 3, 1968, King checked into Memphis's Lorraine Motel, accompanied by Jesse Jackson, Ralph Abernathy, and other SCLC staff members. That night King spoke to over 2,000 people at the Mason Street Temple. "We've got some difficult days ahead, but it really doesn't matter with me now," he told the crowd. "Because I've been to the mountain-top, I won't mind. Like anybody, I would like to live a long life. . . . But I'm not concerned about that now. . . . " Within twenty-four hours, these words made many people think that King had predicted the future.

The next day, preparing to go to dinner, King stepped out onto the balcony of his motel room. Directly below, in a parking lot, Jesse Jackson called up to him and reintroduced King to a local musician friend, Ben Branch. As King turned to go back inside, a shot rang out. An assassin's bullet struck him in the jaw, entered his neck, and severed his spinal cord. Jesse, horrified, watched his hero fall, and with other aides, rushed to his side. Fifteen minutes later an ambulance arrived and carried the stricken King to

St. Joseph's Hospital. But it was too late. At 7:05 P.M., the greatest civil-rights leader in America was pronounced dead. It was the end of an era for the cause of black freedom, and the beginning of a new one for Jesse Jackson.

5

The Big Push

THE TRAGIC MURDER of Martin Luther King, Jr., left the black community in a state of shock. Many poor and forgotten Americans lost all hope for the future. They felt with Dr. King gone there was no one else who could lead them in the struggle against injustice and racism. James Earl Ray, a small-time criminal, was arrested two months after the assassination and later convicted of King's murder. To this day, many people believe that Ray was either falsely accused or part of a larger conspiracy.

Anger, despair, and a thirst for revenge exploded in riots across the nation's urban ghettos. While other members of the SCLC's staff returned to their motel rooms, too stunned to do anything else, Jackson went out and talked to the press and television crews. He felt that someone had to speak out for the SCLC to try and help people cope with this national tragedy.

However, he was not the person most of the other SCLC members would have chosen to serve as spokesperson. At twenty-six, he was only a junior member of the organization. In addition, he was not as close to Dr. King as Ralph Abernathy and others had been. But Jesse felt that if he didn't speak out at this critical moment, no one else would. It was a decision that would make him many friends in the weeks and months ahead, and many enemies as well.

Hours later, as arrangements were being made for the slain leader's funeral, Jesse asked Ralph Abernathy if he could go to Chicago. Abernathy agreed. He thought that Jesse was going to organize people to come down to Memphis for the funeral. However, when he arrived in Chicago Jesse found the city a battleground of rioters and police. Whole neighborhoods had been set afire by their desperate residents. Nine people had died in the violence, and many more were arrested, beaten, or left homeless from the burnings.

Jesse looked around at the destruction and knew he had to speak out. Though he had promised Ralph Abernathy he would not speak to the press again, Jesse felt a higher loyalty to the spirit of his fallen leader. If Martin Luther King, Jr., were alive, Jesse reasoned, he would have urged people to turn away from violence and put their hope in civil disobedience. Jesse felt compelled to do the same.

That morning, he appeared on NBC-TV's *Today Show* wearing the same clothes he had worn in Memphis the day before. Viewers gasped when they saw his sweater soaked in blood, presumably that of King. How the blood got there is still a mystery that has never been fully explained.

"I am calling for nonviolence," he said. "I'm challenging the youth of today to be nonviolent as the greatest expression of faith they can make to Dr. King — to put your rocks down, put your bottles down."

Jackson's statements in Chicago that day were an impassioned cry for reason and restraint. While moderate, older black leaders were silent, and radical, young leaders such as H. Rap Brown were crying for violence and destruction, Jesse's voice spoke out clearly and persuasively for peace and understanding. Still, the SCLC staff members back in Memphis were taken by surprise. They grew even more angry and bitter at this young upstart, who they now saw as an opportunist of the worst sort.

In the aftermath of this dark moment in American history, Jesse Jackson emerged as a figure of stature in the civil-rights struggle. Though Dr. Ralph Abernathy became the new head of the SCLC, it was Jackson who inherited Dr. King's mantle of captivating leadership.

Before he died, Martin Luther King, Jr., had planned the Poor People's Campaign, which would begin with a march to Washington, D.C., the nation's capital. The month after King's death, Jesse Jackson led that march. Together with thousands of poor people, he camped in a park alongside the Lincoln Memorial. Jesse called the camp "resurrection city," but its resurrection was all too brief. A flu epidemic spread through the camp and finally forced people to return home.

In June 1968, Jesse took another step along the path set for him by his dead leader. He was ordained a minister in the Fellowship Missionary Baptist Church in Chicago. A year later he would receive an honorary degree from the Chicago Theological Seminary.

The Reverend Jesse Jackson continued to speak weekly at the Capitol Theatre, but now his speeches were true sermons that strengthened thousands spiritually as well as socially. The more popular Jesse became, the more strained were his relationships with Abernathy and the SCLC leadership. On the surface they remained good friends, working together for a common cause. But beneath the surface there were growing tensions and bitter feelings on both sides.

Now a leader in his own right, Jesse expanded the scope of Operation Breadbasket. He looked for new, exciting ways to capture people's imaginations and build up their self-respect and confidence. As the winter of 1968 approached, Jesse made plans for the celebration of the first "Black Christmas" in Chicago.

The idea was not originally Jesse's, but he put his own unique stamp on it. He urged black shoppers to buy their presents only from black-owned stores. "Rather than looking through the yellow pages," he told them, "you're to start looking through the black pages."

The high point of "Black Christmas" was a parade through the streets of Chicago featuring ninety floats and headed by a horse-drawn wagon. This wagon

Jesse Jackson in 1969. At the time Jackson was working in Chicago as director of "Operation Breadbasket," a program created by Martin Luther King, Jr., that was designed to bring food and money to the urban poor. In 1971, Jesse founded his own organization—PUSH (People United To Serve Humanity).

was, according to Jesse, a somber symbol of "the poverty of the nation's masses." A friend of Jesse's appeared as "Black Soul Saint" from the South Pole, to distinguish him from Santa Claus and the North Pole. The gifts in Soul Saint's sack were not toys but "love, justice, peace, and power." Black Soul Saint wore a black *dashiki,* a loose-fitting robelike African garment, with yellow, red, and green trimmings. These were the national colors of Ghana, which in 1957 was the first modern black African republic to win its freedom from colonialism. European countries such as Great Britain and France had made colonies of the African nations in the late 1800s. Independence in Ghana signalled the beginning of the end for these colonial empires. Jesse wanted black Americans to identify with the self-determination and freedom of their African cousins.

"Black Christmas" was so successful that when spring came, Jesse decided to celebrate a "Black Easter." Another parade was held, this one featuring a big black sheep that symbolized both Jesus Christ, whose resurrection Easter celebrates, and black people, who, like the black sheep, were outcasts of the flock. To drive home this message, a Black Passion Play was staged. Written by a black woman, the drama compared Christ's sufferings to those of black people in history.

These grand events gradually evolved into something far more significant — black fairs, where black businesses could demonstrate and display their products and services to the public. Jesse called them Black Expos.

Chicago's first Black Expo was a showcase for both local and national black businesses, and a few white businesses, too. It was not only a trade fair, but a series of parties, musical concerts, and art exhibitions, all featuring black performers and artists. Each year's Black Expo had a theme that reflected the concerns and aspirations of black Americans. "From Chains to Change" and "See the Dream Coming True" were good examples.

The independent projects Jesse was staging in Chicago further strained his relations with the SCLC. Although still a member of the organization, Jesse was operating increasingly on his own. The tension finally came to a head in 1971, when Ralph Abernathy heard rumors that Jesse would not share the profits of his latest Black Expo with the SCLC. Abernathy took the rumors seriously and came to Chicago to investigate the situation. He found Jesse guiltless of any wrongdoing, but nevertheless punished him for his independence — a sixty-day suspension from the SCLC.

The ambitious young man knew the time had come to move on. He had stayed with the SCLC for three and a half years after Dr. King's death, which he felt was long enough. The SCLC no longer needed him, and he certainly felt he didn't need them. He sent a telegram to Abernathy containing his resignation from the organization. "As we go separate roads," he ended the telegram, "I pray that our goals will remain united. We must feed the hungry, clothe the naked, and set the captive free. Respectfully yours, Jesse Louis Jackson, The Country Preacher."

43

The Country Preacher wasted no time expressing his new independence. A week later, on Christmas Day 1971, he announced the birth of a new organization that would carry on the work he had begun with Operation Breadbasket. He called it "People United to Save Humanity," or PUSH. The word "Save" in the title was later changed to "Serve." The members of this organization, Jesse claimed, would "push for a greater share of economic and political power for poor people in America."

The key word here was economic. With black civil rights basically won in the courts and legislatures, Jesse believed blacks needed to turn their attention to strengthening their earning power. The major goals of PUSH were to help existing black-owned businesses succeed and get new ones started. One way to do this was to convince large, white-owned corporations to give their business to smaller black companies and at the same time hire more black workers.

Boycotts were one option that Jesse had successfully used before to achieve his goals. He was pleasantly surprised to find that this kind of pressure was rarely needed to make a corporation cooperate with PUSH. Big names such as Burger King, the Ford Motor Company, and General Foods respected Jesse's power and sincerity and were freely willing to reach agreements with him. However, Coca Cola needed an extra "push" before they agreed to do business with the organization. When Coke balked at Jesse's proposals, he told his followers to cut down on their Coke drinking. "Don't Choke on Coke" was how he phrased it. In two short weeks Coca Cola was ready to sign an agreement.

Some critics of PUSH claimed it only helped black businesses that were already doing well, and not the poor people who most needed assistance. Jesse responded that *all* blacks benefited from PUSH's successes. Growing black businesses, he claimed, created more jobs, better pay, and a higher standard of living for everyone in the black community. Besides this, he pointed out, PUSH also helped unemployed workers, people on welfare, and Vietnam veterans to collect benefits due them from the government.

Under Jesse's leadership, PUSH grew into a national organization with 60,000 members in sixteen cities. Jesse Jackson had truly arrived as a national figure. In 1970, he appeared on the cover of *Time magazine,* one of the few black Americans to receive this honor. He had become one of the most famous black people in the United States, if not the world.

But there was one particular place where Jesse most wanted to be seen as "somebody." That was his hometown of Greenville, South Carolina. On October 6, 1973, Jesse's wish came true. That was the day that Greenville honored the man who as a boy was not allowed to drink from a "whites-only" water fountain. It declared "Jesse Jackson Day" and celebrated his thirty-second birthday (which actually falls on October 8) with a weekend of tributes and festivities. At one banquet, Jesse looked at the white and black faces around the table and began to cry from happiness. Of all the honors he had received before and since, few have meant as much to him.

As the new year began, it seemed there was no limit to what PUSH and its founder could achieve. Then, with little warning, things started to go wrong. Jesse, who always pushed himself to the limit, became seriously ill. Three years earlier, he had been diagnosed as having sickle-cell anemia, a blood disease that many black Americans are prone to. The disease is caused by the presence of too many abnormal hemoglobin molecules in the red blood cells. These molecules cause the blood cells to change to a sickle shape. The sickle cells clog blood vessels and prevent the free flow of blood. This, in turn, often deprives body tissue of life-giving oxygen. Many black people are born with these abnormal hemoglobin molecules, which are found mostly in people of African heritage.

As Jesse recovered in the hospital from his first bout with the disease, he joked that he welcomed a disease that was African. But three years later, when the disease recurred, it was no laughing matter. Jesse developed pneumonia as well, and his condition was so serious that it took five long stays in the hospital before he fully recovered.

To aggravate his troubles, PUSH's mounting debts became the subject of a government investigation. Around the same time, a number of PUSH aides resigned, complaining that Jesse hadn't given them enough power and responsibility. To make matters even worse, the annual PUSH Expo in Chicago had to be cancelled due to a sudden drop in business.

Discouraged and downhearted, Jesse turned to God and prayed for guidance. After recovering from his illness in late 1974, he traveled to Kansas City, Missouri, to lead a Baptist revival meeting. Soon after, his prayers were answered. As he was driving through Chicago one day, he happened to pass a public high school. What he saw shocked him. Outside, students who should have been in class were smoking, gambling, and dealing drugs. He counted five girls who were pregnant.

Jesse realized how much these young people needed his help and support. If the next generation of black Americans was uneducated, and abused alcohol and drugs, how could it ever expect to prosper? Jesse decided then and there that PUSH needed to take an entirely new direction. In 1976, after months of planning, he founded PUSH for Excellence, or PUSH-Excel, a program aimed at young black students. Jesse wanted to show them there was more to life than drugs, alcohol, and sex.

For the next two years he traveled from high school to high school in America's inner cities, speaking directly to students with a message of hope and self-help. "The victim is not responsible for being down, but he is responsible for getting up," he told them. "Work hard and strive for excellence. You may be in the slums, but don't let the slums be in you."

Jesse spoke frankly about his own youth and his illegitimate birth. Tough young kids who wouldn't listen to their parents or teachers listened to this handsome, young black man. The message he gave them was not that different from one they had heard before: Work hard and be disciplined, and you can succeed in life. But it was the way that Jesse delivered the message that made the difference. He talked to them in language they could understand — the language of the streets and the sports arena. He wasn't afraid to talk as tough to them as they talked to each other.

"Brothers," he said to one group of delinquent boys, "you're not a man because you can kill somebody. You're not a man because you can make a baby. They can make babies through artificial insemination. . . . You're a man only if you can raise a baby, protect a baby, and provide for a baby."

When he was done talking, Jesse presented students with a challenge. He asked them to pledge to spend two hours a night on homework, without letting themselves be distracted by television, radio, or the telephone. "If you spend two hours a night learning to read and write," he said, "you'll be able to slam dunk a thought the way you slam dunk a basketball."

Thousands of young people signed the pledge. So did their parents, who vowed to see that their children put in their two hours nightly at the books. The parents also promised to meet with their children's teachers during the first week of school and keep in communication with them throughout the school year. Teachers and principals took a pledge, too — to take a serious interest in their students' progress and encourage them and offer support. When the students graduated from high school, Jesse arranged for them to be given voter-registration cards along with their diplomas. According to Jesse, being a successful somebody also meant being a responsible citizen who regularly exercised his or her right to vote.

PUSH-Excel had its critics, just as the original PUSH did. Some people said there wasn't enough follow-up on students' academic work. Others said that one inspirational speech from Jesse Jackson wasn't enough to motivate students through four years of high school. While it is true that many students slid back into their old habits, many others improved greatly in school. Jesse's personal appearance made a definite impression on them, something difficult to measure on a graph.

By the beginning of the 1980s, PUSH had regained its status as a national success. PUSH-Excel had become so popular that it was now a separate corporation. Money flowed in from the government and such respected private organizations as the Ford Foundation and the Rockefeller Foundation.

Around this time, Jesse began to feel that he had pushed PUSH as far as he could. Of course, he would continue to help black Americans and poor people of all ages achieve their goals of becoming somebody. But Jesse also recognized that there was a wide world beyond the United States, where even larger problems of poverty, racism, and war loomed. It was these wider horizons, and the new and even greater challenges they held in store, that next captured Jesse's attention and devotion.

49

6

World Ambassador

JESSE JACKSON'S INTEREST in foreign affairs began when he was still a student at the Chicago Theological Seminary. Visitors from abroad would often visit the school and speak to the students about the problems of their homelands. One evening, the United Nations ambassador from Lebanon came to speak. Afterward, Jesse and other students talked late in the night with the ambassador about the situation in the Middle East, a tense and unstable region of the world.

As Jesse became more and more involved in the Civil-Rights Movement and black consciousness, he developed a strong interest in Africa. In the late 1960s, many young black Americans looked to Africa, home of their ancestors, as their spiritual homeland. They called themselves "Afro-Americans," studied African culture, and even dressed in native African clothes. Jesse often wore an African dashiki in public, and sported a bushy "Afro" hairdo.

When he was invited to go to Nigeria, a republic in Western Africa, in 1971, as part of an Afro-American cultural exchange, Jesse jumped at the chance. Jackie and seven-year-old Santita went along with him. The following year Jesse visited Liberia, a West African country founded in 1822 by an American antislavery group as a home for freed black American slaves. Many black Americans felt strong ties with Liberia and some even owned property there. One of the purposes of Jesse's trip was to try and gain dual citizenship for those black Americans who owned property in Liberia so they could live there without giving up their U.S. citizenship. Unfortunately, the plan was not accepted.

Jesse was more successful helping his African brothers in 1973. Five years of drought had created a crisis situation in six West African countries. The lack of rain had drastically reduced the supply of grown food, and as many as ten million people were threatened with starvation. Jesse made a fervent plea to the American people to help. As a result, sixty-five tons of food and medical supplies were donated by both black and white Americans, and many lives were saved.

Jackson next turned his attention to South Africa, where he saw that the mind and soul can suffer just as much as the body. South Africa is home to approximately four million whites, mostly the descendants of Dutch and English colonists, and more than twenty million native blacks. The whites rule the country through apartheid, which means "apart-ness" in

Afrikaans, the official language of South Africa. The laws of apartheid dictate where black South Africans can live, work, and go to school. In effect, apartheid makes blacks prisoners and outcasts in their own land. Indeed, the country's blacks were starving for freedom and the right to live with dignity.

Jesse Jackson was a firm opponent of apartheid and spoke out against this racist policy in the United States. In 1979, Jesse got the opportunity to take his message to South Africa itself. Then-president Jimmy Carter was a friend of Jackson's and helped him get a visa to visit the country.

Jesse arrived in South Africa with Dr. Howard Schomer, his adviser and former professor from the Chicago Theological Seminary. His first speech was a memorable event. It was held at a squatters' camp on the edge of Cape Town, one of South Africa's three capital cities. The tumbledown camp was inhabited by thousands of black South Africans. They were not allowed, under the restrictions of apartheid, to live within the city limits. Although the weather was rainy and mud covered the ground, thousands of blacks came to hear the famous preacher from America. Their enthusiasm was reflected in a banner above the speaker's platform, which read: "Welcome Reverend Jesse Jackson, distinguished son of Mother Africa." Jesse's speech was translated into Bantu, an African tribal language, and his words of support and encouragement reached the hearts of his listeners. When he finished, they responded not with applause but with joyful singing.

At Soweto, a black township near the city of Johannesburg, Jackson donned a native straw hat and a zebra-skin cloak to illustrate his bond with black South Africans. "I may be black, I may be poor," he told a crowd of 10,000, "I may have lost hope, but I am God's child!" He urged them to fight apartheid through civil disobedience, the same method that had worked so well for blacks in the United States in the 1950s and 1960s. The crowd went wild with enthusiasm, lifted a surprised Jackson on their shoulders, and carried him aloft in celebration of his support.

Jesse returned to the United States determined to raise America's consciousness about apartheid. He urged the government and private businesses to end their financial relationships with the South African government. At first, many corporations resisted this pressure. They thought that taking their investments out of that country would mean losing money. They also said that doing so would deprive blacks of sorely needed jobs. But gradually nearly all of them ended their financial and business links to South Africa, letting the government know that they, too, were opposed to apartheid.

In later years, Jesse would lead protest rallies at the South African embassy and consular offices in Washington, D.C., New York, and Chicago. He also participated in demonstrations in several European countries.

While a majority of Americans supported Jackson's stand against South Africa, many opposed him when he took another stand in international politics. For many years, Jews and Arabs in the Middle East had been enemies, fighting over land and their religious and cultural differences. With the creation of Israel, a Jewish state, in 1948, this rivalry intensified. The United States had been a firm supporter of Israel since its founding. Many American Jews had settled in Israel, and many more felt strong ties with the new nation and its democratic values.

Jesse respected Israel's right to exist, but felt strongly sympathetic toward the Arabs who had been left displaced or homeless by the establishment of Israel. He felt it was unfair that the United States should ignore these people's needs. He saw these Arabs as forgotten people who needed a champion, just as the poor people of the United States needed one. One way to help them, Jackson thought, would be to gain acceptance in the United States and Israel for the Palestine Liberation Organization (PLO). This was one of the major purposes of his September 1979 tour of Israel, Lebanon, Jordan, Syria, and Egypt.

The PLO represented the rights of Palestinian Arabs in the Middle East. However, many Americans and Israelis did not like the PLO's tactics, which included violent acts against civilian targets to publicize the Palestinian cause. Many Palestinians were also repulsed by the violence. Others supported the acts as necessary evils in the fight for justice. Thus, Jesse Jackson's pro-Arab stand was extremely controversial.

Jesse found few friends when he arrived in Israel. Most Israeli leaders refused to meet with him. One exception was Mayor Teddy Kollek of Jerusalem,

55

known as a liberal thinker. To show that he was not an enemy of the Jewish people, Jesse donned a skullcap and prayed at the Western Wall, Judaism's holiest site. (The Western Wall, sometimes called the Wailing Wall, was once part of a vast temple complex that was destroyed in A.D. 70.) However, some Jews objected when he compared the Nazi extermination of six million Jews in World War II with the suffering of blacks under slavery in the United States. They felt that the Holocaust, as it is known, was unique in the history of human suffering.

In Beirut, Lebanon, Jackson met with PLO leader Yasir Arafat. A photograph of Jackson warmly embracing Arafat appeared on newspaper front pages across America and earned Jesse sharp criticism from many people. They saw his friendliness toward Arafat as an acceptance of terrorism. Jesse's reputation with many Jews would remain tarnished for a long time.

In Cairo, Egypt, Jesse met with Egyptian President Anwar el-Sadat, who shared his concern about the hostilities between Jews and Arabs. Sadat asked Jackson to carry a message back to Arafat, calling for a cease-fire between Israelis and Arabs. (Sadat and Arafat were not on speaking terms because of Egypt's peace treaty with Israel, signed earlier in the year.) Arafat refused Sadat's request, but his relationship with Jesse remained friendly. He visited Jackson when Jesse entered a Beirut hospital to be treated for a stomach ailment.

Peace in the Middle East has always been an elusive goal, and Jackson's first attempts at internation-

Jackson with Archbishop bishop Desmond Tutu, a leading South African religious and political figure, at the Washington Cathedral in Washington, D.C., December 1984. Both men have denounced South Africa's policy of apartheid, or racial segregation, and have challenged the U.S. government to work harder to change that country's discriminatory actions.

al diplomacy were not very successful. However, a few years later he was to surprise the nation and the world with a personal diplomatic victory.

In December 1983, a U.S. Navy fighter plane, part of an American peacekeeping force in the Middle East, was shot down over Lebanon during a bombing raid. (American forces had been drawn reluctantly into the local fighting.) The pilot died in the crash, but the twenty-seven-year-old navigator/bombardier, Lt. Robert O. Goodman, a black American, was taken as a "prisoner of war" by Syria. President Ronald Reagan attempted to negotiate with Syria for Goodman's release, but with no success. Syrian relations with the United States were strained for several reasons relating to the overall situation in the Middle East.

Jackson took a personal interest in the case. He felt he might have a chance to succeed where the government had failed. In his 1979 tour, he had met and established friendly ties with Syrian President Hafez al-Assad. Perhaps, thought Jesse, Assad could be convinced, in a one-on-one meeting, to release Goodman on humanitarian grounds. At Assad's invitation, Jesse announced his plans to fly to Syria in late December. "We must go on faith," he explained just before his departure. "I certainly hope to bring Lt. Goodman back. . . . We're doing the right thing."

The Reagan administration didn't agree with this approach, and took a dim view of Jackson's personal diplomatic mission. They claimed he was out of his element in international negotiations, and felt he had no right to involve himself in what should have been the State Department's job. They thought he might endanger ongoing negotiations. They feared that Assad could deliver a diplomatic snub to the United States by allowing a citizen to succeed where the president had failed. Finally, they felt that Jackson could put his own life, and that of Goodman's, in danger.

Jesse knew the risks involved, but he also had faith and confidence in his abilities to deal with the Syrian president. He arrived in Syria on December 29 with a small entourage, and waited several days for a meeting with Assad. New Year's Day came and went with still no word. Jesse had planned to leave the country on January 2, 1984, but now, with growing apprehension, he delayed his departure. "We would rather wait here in Syria with the possibility of getting Robert Goodman free than be back home hoping it would happen," he told reporters.

Finally, on January 3, Jackson and Assad met near Damascus, Syria's capital. Jesse pleaded his case eloquently, telling the Syrian president that it was only humane that he release the American flyer, regardless of how he felt about the United States policy that had brought Goodman there. He also pointed out that if Goodman remained a prisoner, the U.S. government could increase the number of U.S. military flights over Syria.

Jesse met with the Syrian foreign minister the following day, and emerged from this meeting with a wide smile and good news. "Our prayers have been answered," Jesse told the press. Goodman was being released unconditionally into his custody by the Syr-

59

ians. Later that same day, Jackson and Goodman left Syria, flying first to West Germany and then on to Andrews Air Force Base in Maryland.

Jesse, who had left the states facing public doubts about his mission, returned home a hero. President Reagan himself welcomed the pair home and personally thanked Jackson for his efforts. "Jackson has earned our gratitude and our admiration," read an official White House statement.

Jesse Jackson had proved to the world that he was a skillful diplomat who could negotiate successfully with world leaders. This new image couldn't have come at a better time for the civil-rights leader. Only a month earlier Jesse had announced his candidacy for the Democratic party's presidential nomination. Jesse Jackson, who had never previously held elective office, was running for president. How he came to make this momentous decision had its roots in another election that year — the race for mayor in Jesse's home base of Chicago.

7

Change in Chicago

IN 1976, THE long struggle between the mayor of Chicago and black activists came to an end. Mayor Richard J. Daley, who had single-handedly run the city of Chicago for more than two decades, died. Daley had stubbornly resisted the efforts of Martin Luther King, Jr., and Jesse Jackson after him, to give blacks a voice in city government. But with his passing, Jesse Jackson and other black leaders were hopeful the system would change.

When Democrat Jane Byrne won a surprise victory in the 1979 mayoral election, those hopes seemed justified. Byrne had campaigned as a reformer, and seemed genuinely concerned about Chicago's blacks. For a time, she and her husband had lived in a crime-ridden housing project on the South Side to illustrate her concern for the poor and the troubled.

But other acts of Mayor Byrne's were not as well received by Chicago's blacks. Her appointment of three whites to Chicago's Housing Board took the balance of power away from the blacks on the Board. This move was seen as insensitive. Her plan for a Chicago Fest that would be a cultural celebration of the city seemed aimed primarily at middle-class whites. Contributions to the arts by blacks, who made up forty percent of the city's population, seemed strangely overlooked.

One Sunday morning in 1983, Jesse Jackson, the most famous black resident of Chicago, was the guest on a live talk show on a local black radio station. He was there to field comments, complaints, and questions from listeners. One woman criticized Mayor Byrne's shabby treatment of blacks and suggested the black community boycott the upcoming Chicago Fest. Jesse, who was no stranger to boycotts and their effectiveness, agreed that this was a good idea. Later that same day, after conferring with other black leaders, he went back on the air and officially called for the boycott.

The response surprised even him. The anger and frustration at decades of neglect and abuse by the city's politicians exploded in the black community. The boycott was a resounding success. Black Chicagoans spoke out bitterly and forcefully in public against Mayor Byrne. However, Jackson realized quickly that a boycott alone was not enough. A positive, productive way had to be found to vent these intense feelings. Political action was needed.

Jackson believed that the best way to change the system and make politicians responsive to people's needs was through the ballot box. But thousands of blacks were indifferent, and weren't even registered to vote. So Jesse began the most ambitious voter-registration drive of his career. Voter registration tables were set up in churches, unemployment offices, and even fast-food restaurants. Anywhere black people congregated, Jesse and his PUSH staff could be found. In a short time, the drive had added as many as 150,000 new blacks to the city's voting rolls.

The strength of the boycott and the effectiveness of the voting drive gave Mayor Byrne, who was running for reelection, reason to be concerned. She had not been successful at balancing the needs of poor blacks and middle-class whites in Chicago. In fact, blacks felt they had been neglected by her administration. The early promises of her reform campaign only made their disappointment and frustration all the greater.

Another politician gained strength and confidence from the anger of black voters. He was Congressman Harold Washington, one of Chicago's most prominent black leaders. Washington had run for mayor in a special election following Daley's death in 1977 but received only eleven percent of the vote. Now, however, with enlarged rolls of black voters and their dissatisfaction with Mayor Byrne, Washington felt he might have a chance of winning in 1983. If he did, he would become the first black mayor in Chicago history, and one of the most powerful black politicians in the country.

When Washington entered his name in the Democratic primary for mayor, he found himself facing not only Mayor Byrne, but Mayor Daley's son, Richard M. Daley. The two white candidates had strong backing

from national figures in the Democratic party. Senator Ted Kennedy of Massachusetts had endorsed
Byrne, while former Vice-President Walter Mondale
had come out for Richard Daley. But Harold Washington had Jesse Jackson in his corner, and Jesse
worked for his candidate with a zeal that no one else
could match. He praised Washington on radio, television, and from church pulpits all across the city. He
stepped up his voter-registration drive. By election
night, there were 635,000 blacks registered to vote.
This was an incredible statistic, considering that
most mayoral elections in the city only brought out
about 850,000 voters overall!

Washington himself proved to be a forceful, impressive candidate. He dominated televised debates,
running rings around Daley and attacking Mayor
Byrne on her record. He promised, if elected, to end
what he called the "racism that permeates all aspects
of Chicago's government." The last poll taken before
the primary showed Byrne ahead of Washington by
nine percentage points. But on election day, Daley
and Byrne split the white vote, allowing Washington
to win by a slim margin. Six out of seven blacks had
voted for Washington. That had made all the difference.

It was a night of triumph for black Chicago, Harold
Washington, and Jesse Jackson. The Daley Democratic "machine" had, for the first time ever, been
broken. The forgotten blacks of Chicago would finally have a voice in how their city, and lives, were run.
As Jesse exclaimed on television when the final vote
was in, "Our time has come!"

Washington easily won the November general election against Republican candidate Bernard Epton, a millionaire businessman. Jesse, evaluating the meaning of the victory, realized that black people, when motivated to action, could be a political force to be reckoned with. In his years with Operation Breadbasket and PUSH, Jesse showed that black people supporting black businesses led to more economic power for all blacks. By the same principle, he reasoned, black voters supporting and electing black politicians would give blacks more political power than they had ever had before. If black voters could make a Harold Washington the mayor of Chicago, why couldn't they do the same for a black running for governor, senator, or even president?

In September 1983, with the election all but won, Jesse saw his work in Chicago finished for the moment. He took a leave of absence from PUSH and left town. His stated reasons for leaving were to travel and pursue the issue of voter registration. But the real reason was that he was about to test the waters to see if a black man — Jesse himself — could gather enough support to run for the highest elective office in the land — the presidency of the United States.

8

Jesse for President!

AN IMPORTANT PART of the American Dream is the belief that anyone in this country — no matter who he or she is — can grow up to be president. It is a dream that a number of Americans no longer believe in. They say that those who might otherwise make excellent leaders lack the money and power required to mount a campaign for president. However, even among those people who cling to the dream, it is doubtful they would believe that a black person — whoever he or she was — could be elected President of the United States.

True, black Congresswoman Shirley Chisholm ran for the Democratic presidential nomination in 1972. Despite a courageous and well-publicized campaign, she won few votes. The sad truth was that Shirley Chisholm never had a serious shot at the nomination, and she knew it. The voters were not ready to accept a black and a woman as a candidate. Eleven years later, Jesse Jackson felt the situation had changed. The election of Harold Washington in Chicago, Tom Bradley in Los Angeles, and other black mayors in major American cities had proved it. Their successes told Jesse that he could seriously aspire to be president.

Jackson's "flirting" with the idea of running for president was a matter of public attention and discussion. Many people wondered why a man who had never held an elective office before in his life wanted to run for president. The answers varied.

Certainly Jackson wanted to carry on his crusade to help the poor and forgotten people of the United States. The powerful position of president of the United States would allow him to do that better than any other.

In addition, running for president, even if he didn't win, was a fine way to convey his message to the American public. He could tell the nation during the campaign about how he felt on the issues of poverty and racism, the economy and the military. He could describe policies and programs that he felt would help to improve the lives of millions of Americans.

Jesse was also a born speaker, a natural showman, a man who loved to meet people and work hard eighteen to twenty hours a day. Therefore, campaigning for president was something he could actually look forward to with joy and enthusiasm. Other politicians commonly saw running for president as extremely difficult and stressful.

Finally, ambition must have played a part in Jesse's decision to run. Maybe it was inevitable that the little boy from Greenville who yearned to be somebody would one day aspire to be the biggest somebody in the Western World — the president of the United States.

Whatever his reasons, Jesse took his time in announcing his decision, and talked it over with his family and friends before declaring his candidacy. Meanwhile, seven other Democrats, all of them white and all of them established politicians, were already off and running for the nomination.

On November 2, 1983, Jesse came to Washington to witness the signing by President Ronald Reagan of a new law that established Martin Luther King, Jr.'s birthday as a national holiday. It was a law that Jesse had advocated for some time. One day later, he spoke at a rally of 2,500 supporters at Washington Convention Hall. He told the enthusiastic crowd that the country's Democratic leadership had been "too silent and too passive" during Reagan's four years as President. He sharply criticized Reagan's policies as "pro-rich, pro-aristocratic, pro-agribusiness, pro-military, and pro-big business." He said a new leader was needed, someone who would stand up for the rights of "the poor and dispossessed of the nation." Then, to roars of approval, he said, "I am announcing today that I am a candidate for president." Holding his hands high in the air, he proclaimed, "These hands that picked cotton can pick the next president of the United States!"

But the road to the White House would be an uphill struggle every step of the way for the new candidate. Being black was only one of a number of problems he faced. Jesse had little money, no strong political organization to run a national campaign, and no experienced staff people to advise him. Perhaps worst of all, the black leadership of America was sharply divided in its support for Jesse. Some leaders, such as Ralph Abernathy, had personal reasons for not supporting him. Others simply felt that Jesse's candidacy would split the Democratic party and help Republican Ronald Reagan win a second term as President. The Reagan administration had cut many federal programs to the poor and needy, while at the same time increasing military spending. Returning the President to office for another four years was the last thing most black leaders wanted. In essence, their dislike of Reagan and his policies was stronger than their desire for a black nominee. They also felt that a black could not win a general election.

Important big-city black mayors such as Andrew Young of Atlanta, Tom Bradley of Los Angeles, and Coleman Young of Detroit supported a white candidate, former Vice-President Walter Mondale of Minnesota. Even Coretta Scott King, the widow of Martin Luther King, Jr., endorsed Mondale. But Jesse refused to let these serious drawbacks dampen his spirits. "If you run, you might lose," he admitted. "But if you don't run, you're guaranteed to lose."

Jesse called his constituency a "Rainbow Coalition" made up of those Americans "left naked before the Lord in the wintertime." They included not only blacks and the poor, but also Hispanics, Asians, the elderly, women, and small farmers. All these groups had been forgotten, Jesse claimed, by the

Reagan administration and by rank-and-file Democrats. Fortunately, they all had a place in the Rainbow Coalition, a coalition which knew no color line and whose slogan was: "Red, yellow, brown, black, and white — we're all precious in God's sight."

It was a powerful message. But without money to buy commercial time on television, how was Jesse going to get the message to the voters? The answer was a simple one. Why buy media time, he reasoned, when you could get it for free on the six o'clock news? Indeed, Jesse made news wherever he went. His speeches were always eloquent, interesting, and quotable. He himself was a handsome, passionate, and exciting candidate. Polls showed that, compared to Jesse, the other seven Democratic candidates were bland, if not downright boring.

The race for the nomination was to take place in a long series of state presidential primary elections beginning in March. With the release of Lt. Goodman in January, Jesse's campaign really took off. He was big news now, and reporters followed him every step along the campaign trail. In one bold move, he had proven he was as knowledgeable and effective on the international scene as on the national scene.

But just as everything seemed to be going right for candidate Jackson, everything suddenly went wrong. Jesse made some serious errors in judgment that hurt his credibility. In February, Milton Coleman, a black reporter for *The Washington Post,* claimed that Jesse, in a private conversation, had made a negative remark about Jewish people and, particularly, Jews living in New York City. The story couldn't have broken at a more terrible time — just eight days before the first presidential primary in New Hampshire. Jesse waited too long to admit that he had made the remark. When he finally did, he did his best to make amends, journeying to a Jewish synagogue in Manchester, New Hampshire, to offer a public apology. "It was not in the spirit of meanness," he explained, "but an off-color remark having no bearing on religion or politics." As "innocent and unintended" as the remark was, he had to admit "it was wrong."

Despite the apology, the incident hurt him badly in the first primary. Jesse finished fourth with only five percent of the vote, tying former South Dakota Senator George McGovern and, ironically, President Reagan, who was a Democratic write-in candidate. But if Jesse came out of New Hampshire looking bad, other candidates looked worse. Three of them did so poorly with the voters that they dropped out of the race. They were former Governor Reubin Askew of Florida, and Senators Alan Cranston of California and Ernest Hollings from Jesse's home state of South Carolina.

Surprisingly, the big winner in New Hampshire was not Walter Mondale, the favored front-runner, but Senator Gary Hart of Colorado. Hart, who offered voters "new ideas" and a Kennedy-like image, beat Mondale by nine percentage points. Political experts were already saying the Democratic race was narrowing down to these two men.

Meanwhile, Jesse Jackson's problems were only beginning. Louis Farrakhan, one of his friends and supporters, was intensifying Jesse's difficulties with Jewish voters. Farrakhan was the leader of the Nation of Islam, a splinter group of the Black Muslims. He was an extremist who, unlike Jesse and other responsible black leaders, preached hatred against whites. He claimed the best way to fight racism was for black Americans to form their own separate society.

After the story broke about Jackson's Jewish remark, Farrakhan made a public death threat against the reporter, Milton Coleman. Jesse came out strongly against Farrakhan's statements, but failed to completely disavow his former friend. He was criticized for this, although he, in turn, criticized the media for holding him accountable for what Farrakhan said and did.

Through it all, Jesse continued to campaign hard across the country. "Super Tuesday" was rapidly approaching. With five primaries and several caucuses, this was the biggest day of the primary season. Jesse surprised nearly everyone on Super Tuesday by winning major blocks of voters in three Southern states: twenty-one percent of the votes in Georgia, over nineteen percent in Alabama, and nearly thirteen percent in Florida. This strong showing not only established Jesse as a serious candidate who could win votes, but preserved his eligibility for federal campaign funds. (Under the Federal Election Campaign Reform Act of 1984, each presidential candidate for the nomination of a major party is eligible for up to $5 million in federal funds if he or she can attain enough primary votes. This measure was passed in reaction to controversy surrounding private contributions to presidential candidates.)

When the dust of Super Tuesday settled, there were only three candidates left standing on their feet — Mondale, Hart, and Jackson. George McGovern, and Ohio senator and former astronaut John Glenn had dropped out after poor showings.

With the field narrowed down, Jesse's support grew, especially in states with large urban black populations. Mondale was the traditional candidate of the labor unions and other special-interest groups. Hart attracted so-called "yuppies," young urban professionals. Jackson reached out to America's underclass — the poor and minorities. He spoke about real social change in America, which the other candidates ignored or merely paid lip service to. He stood for ideals, and that made him unique as a candidate. Even those Democrats who didn't support Jesse had to acknowledge this and respect him for it.

While Jesse continued to run third in a three-man race, he was picking up steam, particularly among black voters. In the Illinois primary, he won seventy-nine percent of the black vote and twenty-one percent of the total vote. In New York he won nearly ninety percent of the black vote and ended up less than two percent behind Gary Hart in the total vote count. He also took a respectable thirty-four percent of the Hispanic vote and six percent of the white vote. But his real triumph came in Pennsylvania. He was not expected to do well in the state because Philadelphia Mayor Wilson Goode strongly supported Mondale. Since Goode was black, this was seen as damaging for Jackson. But when the votes were counted, Jesse had won not only in Philadelphia but had received seventy-five percent of the black vote statewide. The candidate was ecstatic. "Without one television commercial, without one newspaper ad — a poor campaign and a rich message," he exclaimed. "We're moving up."

Poor was an appropriate word to describe the Jackson campaign. While Mondale and Hart had expensive fund-raising dinners, Jesse was reduced to passing the collection plate for pocket change at black churches. Jesse's traveling entourage was small, and reporters had to be charged to fly on his campaign airplane. The candidate avoided expensive hotel bills by staying at the homes of friends and supporters whenever he could.

Perhaps his most interesting overnight stay on the campaign trail was in a small town near Pittsburgh, Pennsylvania. He was invited to spend the night at the modest home of a white unemployed steelworker. The neighbors must have been startled when Jesse and his family arrived around midnight, accompanied by a string of police cars. Jesse and his wife Jackie slept on a water bed in the master bedroom, while their host and his wife made do on couches in the living room.

Jesse's family also worked hard to get out the vote. Jackie spoke to crowds in churches all across America and sometimes even on street corners. Besides repeating her husband's stand on foreign and domestic policy, she spoke out for women's rights, especially the passing of the Equal Rights Amendment to the Constitution. The four eldest Jackson children — Jesse's family now included five children — did their part as well. Jesse, Jr., and Jonathan Luther, both high school seniors, spoke to youth groups and others every weekend. They and their sister Santita were old political pros, having stood by their dad on picket lines and in demonstrations for years. Thirteen-year-old Yusef was new to the political scene, but made up for her inexperience with typical Jackson enthusiasm.

On May 1, Jesse Jackson won his first primary by amassing sixty-seven percent of the votes in the District of Columbia. Just four days later he won the Louisiana primary with forty-three percent of the vote. These victories were no accident, for Jesse was campaigning hard, sometimes speaking up to five times a day.

The promise of May, however, soon gave way to the grim realities of June. The powerful Democratic machine behind Walter Mondale overwhelmed the passionate but amateur Jackson campaign. Early that month, it was clear to everyone, even Jesse, that Mondale had enough convention delegates behind him to win the nomination at the July convention. In the five primaries held on June 5, Jesse placed last in all, including the all-important contest in California. However, Jesse wasn't about to call it quits. With over 380 delegates pledged to support him, he could still be a major player at the convention. He felt he could influence the party's platform and help make the Mondale candidacy more sensitive to the needs of disadvantaged Americans.

After returning to South Carolina for a brief rest, Jesse took off on a six-day tour of Latin America. He met with President Jose Napolean Duarte of El Salvador, President Daniel Ortega of Nicaragua, and Fidel Castro of Cuba. This was no publicity tour without substance. Rather, every stop on Jackson's visit was an important one. He brought President Duarte peace proposals from El Salvador's left-wing guerilla army. He showed his support for President Ortega's Sandinista government, which the Reagan administration opposed and fought against by backing a rebel force known as the "contras." In Cuba, Jackson's meeting with Castro led to the release of forty-eight political prisoners, something the United States government, which opposed Castro's communist government, was not able to achieve.

While Jesse was out of the country demonstrating his abilities as a foreign diplomat, back home Louis Farrakhan was stirring up more trouble for him. Farrakhan had given a speech in which he called Judaism a "gutter religion" and claimed the United States had entered into a "criminal conspiracy" in its strong support for Israel. This time Jesse did not hedge in his criticism of the Black Muslim leader. He denounced Farrakhan's words as "reprehensible and morally indefensible."

On June 12 the last primary was held in North Dakota. The three Democratic candidates breathed a sigh of relief. At last, the long, demanding primary season was over. The final count of delegates gave Walter Mondale the majority he needed for the nomination — 2,191 delegates. Gary Hart wound up with

1,200, Jesse with 465. Jesse may have lost, but his loss was an impressive one. He began the campaign late and with few resources. His total campaign expenditures of $6.4 million were a fourth of what Mondale spent and less than half of Hart's expenses. Still, Jackson won 3.5 million votes in the primaries and brought in about a million new voters through his campaign and voter registration drives. He had proven to a doubting public that a black man could run for president and be taken seriously. It was an astonishing achievement.

Jesse came to San Francisco, site of the Democratic convention, in mid-July, expecting to exercise some real clout. He was sorely disappointed. His platform proposals for a twenty-percent cut in military spending and a turnaround in Middle East policy were flatly rejected on the convention floor. So was his proposal to eliminate unfair primary practices in southern states that prevented many minority candidates from being elected.

Many Democrats feared that an unhappy Jackson would bolt and form his own party. Several presidential hopefuls in the past had done this and doomed the Democrats to defeat by dividing the party. But Jesse Jackson didn't see himself as a spoiler. He had entered this presidential race to make America aware of its underprivileged citizens and to bring these people into the mainstream, not exclude them further from it. He would work within the system, as did his role model, Martin Luther King, Jr.

On July 17, 1984, Jesse delivered a speech to the convention that was hailed as one of the greatest speeches in American political history, topped only by one he made at another convention four years later. He talked about the Democratic Party, the American Dream, and what he had learned in the past eleven months.

"This campaign has taught me much," he told the delegates and ninety million television viewers, "that leaders must be tough enough to fight, tender enough to cry, human enough to make mistakes, humble enough to admit them, strong enough to absorb the pain, and resilient enough to bounce back and keep on moving. For leaders, the pain is often intense. But you must smile through your tears and keep moving with the faith that there is a brighter side somewhere. . . . If in my low moments, in word, deed, or attitude, through some error of temper, taste, or tone, I have caused anyone discomfort, created pain, or revived someone's fears, that was not my truest self. . . . I am not a perfect servant. I am a public servant doing my best against the odds. As I develop and serve, be patient. God is not finished with me yet."

God wasn't finished with Jesse Jackson. Neither were the American people.

9

Conscience of a Nation

O UR TIME HAS come!" Jesse Jackson declared
to the Democrats at their convention in San
Francisco. But the presidential election of
1984 proved him wrong, at least this time around.
Ronald Reagan was still a very popular president,
and Walter Mondale had a hard time damaging his
image, despite strong performances in two televised
debates. Jesse campaigned hard for Mondale, but it
did not improve the Democratic candidate's chances
when Election Day came in November. The Democrats suffered a crushing defeat. Mondale lost every
state but Minnesota, his home state, and the District
of Columbia. Ronald Reagan had easily won a second
term as President.

The self-doubts and defeatism felt by many Democrats were not shared by Jesse Jackson. In truth, he
had nothing to be sorry for. The public defeat of his
party was, ironically, a personal victory for him. He

had fought a strong campaign for the nomination and had supported the chosen candidate vigorously right up until Election Day. He was now ready to return to the issues closest to his heart — the poor and their problems.

Jackson divided his time between working for PUSH in Chicago and further developing his Rainbow Coalition from an office in Washington, D.C. He returned to his public pulpit Saturday mornings in Chicago, getting back in touch with the people who knew him best and who shared his dreams and hopes for America. He vowed to carry on his drive for voter registration and also promised to keep the causes he believed in alive and on the minds of the Reagan administration. Although his party was out of power, he felt far from powerless. Jesse Jackson saw himself as the conscience of his country, now more than ever. Perhaps a member of Jackson's staff put it best: "Jesse is like the watchdog that's always there. He's on top of everything. He'll remind you if the country has done something wrong."

In January 1985, in response to the official presidential inauguration ceremonies, Jesse led a "counter-inaugural" march right by the White House. This was followed by a prayer vigil. Two months later, Jesse joined other civil-rights leaders in an emotional recreation of the civil-rights march from Selma to Montgomery, Alabama, that had taken place exactly twenty years before. Much had changed in America in those two decades. Much had changed for Jesse Jackson, too. He had gone from being one of thousands of black student protesters to a presidential hopeful. It had been a long and exciting journey, but it was far from over. There were more battles to be fought and won, and Jesse threw himself into the fight with characteristic energy and fervor.

While busy on the home front, Jesse did not forget about world problems. In April, he attended a large antiapartheid demonstration at the South African Embassy in Washington, where he was arrested along with other demonstrators, and briefly sent to jail. In May he visited France and West Germany. During the trip Jesse expressed sympathy for the Jews who suffered and died by the millions in Europe during World War II. He was reaching out to Jews, trying to break down the barriers that had arisen during the 1984 campaign. Returning to the states, he spoke of the "community of suffering" he felt black Americans and Jewish people shared.

But Jackson wasn't merely paying lip service to the people he had offended. He backed his words with decisive action. When President Reagan journeyed to Geneva, Switzerland, to meet with the new Soviet leader, Mikhail Gorbachev, Jesse went to Geneva, too. He met with Gorbachev and confronted him on the issue of Soviet Jewry. Discrimination against Soviet Jews prompts many to want to leave the Soviet Union and live instead in Israel or the United States. Jackson appealed to the Soviet leader to allow more Soviet Jews to emigrate. The conscience of a nation was becoming the conscience of the world as well.

January 20, 1986, marked the first national observance of Martin Luther King Day. Instead of simply honoring his late friend and mentor, Jesse used the occasion to criticize the Reagan administration. He took the President and other Republicans to task for honoring King in death while largely ignoring him while he was alive. Many Americans, Jackson believed, were guilty of viewing Dr. King as a "nonthreatening dreamer." Jesse quickly reminded them that King was "not assassinated for dreaming" but for forcing white America to face the unpleasant truths of racism and prejudice.

A few months later, at a three-day conference in Chicago, Jesse officially announced the formation of a new National Rainbow Coalition. He promised that it would be a "progressive force" within the Democratic Party. Did this mean he was gearing up for another try for the presidential nomination in 1988? Jesse wouldn't commit himself, but many people saw his announcement as the unofficial beginning of another presidential campaign.

However, in the 1986 midterm elections, Jesse was a supporter and not a candidate. He campaigned forcefully for a number of Democratic candidates running for state and local offices. All the candidates he supported were white, and many hadn't supported him for president two years earlier. Why was he helping them now? some of his supporters wondered. "I'm trying to build a Rainbow Coalition," Jesse reminded them. "Maybe the next time, they'll return the favor."

In August, he returned to Africa for a seventeen-day tour of eight countries. He was accompanied by educators, businesspeople, and other black leaders.

His ties to what he saw as the homeland of all former slaves and their descendants were stronger than ever. However, when Anglican Bishop Desmond Tutu of South Africa, a leader in the fight against apartheid, invited him to his inauguration as archbishop, Jesse regretfully declined. The South African authorities did not want another visit from the American civil-rights leader. They put heavy restrictions on his visa, limiting where he could go and what he could do. Jesse wisely decided he could do little good in going at that time, and stayed home.

Meanwhile, many people were asking him what his intentions were with the Rainbow Coalition. Was he going to create a permanent political base with it? "I will remain active in the forefront of our quest for freedom and human dignity," he answered, "so long as I live and am able of mind and body." As 1987 loomed ahead, it was clear that the "forefront" would once again take him on the quest for the presidency. Only this time the quest would turn out to be a very different one.

10

Win, Jesse, Win!

JESSE JACKSON OPENED a campaign office in Iowa on March 19, 1987, and seemed about to become a presidential candidate for the second time. Some people wondered why. He had proven that a black man could be a legitimate candidate for president in 1984, but he had no real chance of winning then. Why should he think he had any more of a chance of taking the Democratic nomination in 1988?

What these people didn't realize was that American politics had changed a lot in four years. Walter Mondale, the Democratic candidate in 1984, had quickly faded from the scene after his disastrous defeat to Ronald Reagan. No major contender in the party had since appeared to take his place. Of the seven declared Democratic candidates, none of them was a household word or had a national following, except for Gary Hart and Jesse Jackson.

In addition, many black politicians who had supported Mondale four years earlier were now ready to join the ranks of Jackson supporters. They were impressed by the eighty percent of the black vote Jesse had won in the 1984 primaries. Another attraction was Jesse's liberal stand, which set him apart from the other cautiously moderate candidates.

Most important of all, many white, middle-class voters had not benefited from eight years of Reagan "prosperity." Thousands of blue-collar workers in the big cities were out of work and angry. Thousands of farmers in the heartland were facing bankruptcy and the loss of their farms. Jesse Jackson's message of sharing America's wealth and helping the needy didn't sound as radical to them now as it had four years earlier.

Jackson thus saw an opportunity to broaden his support. Where he was once a minority candidate mainly representing blacks and the poor, now he made a serious effort to enter the mainstream of American politics. He cut his hair and dressed a little more conservatively. He toned down his attack on white racism in America. He realized that if he wanted to be president, he would have to appeal to many different groups of Americans and show them he could be a leader to them all. He had grown and matured as both a politician and human being since 1984. Then, his Rainbow Coalition of supporters was an ideal he never attained. Now, he was determined to make it a reality.

None of this meant he was going to be any less outspoken than he had been in the past. While the other candidates avoided controversy, Jesse was unafraid to take a strong stand on issues he believed in, no matter how unpopular his position. He spoke out firmly against the spread of handguns. He fervently attacked American businesses that were going abroad to build factories. He felt this would take jobs away from American workers. He continued his support for a Palestinian homeland and for an end to apartheid in South Africa.

"We must stop the flow of drugs into our country and stop the flow of jobs out of it," he told supporters in a campaign kickoff speech.

"Let's stop *mergin'* corporations, *purgin'* workers," he told truck drivers at the annual Teamsters Convention. "Let's shift to *reinvestment in America!*"

"If we can bail out Chrysler and we can bail out New York City, both of which we should have done," he told Midwest farmers, "then we can and should bail out the family farmer."

"He's talking the language that working people want to hear, regardless of race," pointed out James Albright of the American Federation of Labor/Congress of Industrial Organizations, in Alabama.

By November 1987, Jesse Jackson, the underdog of 1984, was the front-runner in the Democratic polls. "From the back of the bus to the front of the polls. That's a long way, don't you think?" the candidate crowed to reporters.

The early primaries in Iowa and New Hampshire, in March 1988, would present Jesse with his first major challenge in the campaign. Neither state had many black voters. If he could do well here, it was thought, that would prove he could appeal to the white middle class whom he needed to be taken seriously as a potential winner.

Jackson concentrated his campaign efforts on Iowa, the less conservative state, and won a respectable, if not impressive, eleven percent of the votes cast. He got only eight percent in New Hampshire. But he did far better in two other New England states shortly after, earning twenty-seven percent of the vote in Vermont and thirty-one percent in Maine. Again, both states had few blacks. The Jackson campaign was starting to build momentum.

"Six months ago, no one was talking about his winning," said political expert Robert Bechel. "People are beginning to talk about it in whispers late at night." Bechel's comment highlighted a real concern for the Democratic party. Some Democrats feared the possibility of Jackson being nominated for president. With Ronald Reagan leaving the White House after two terms, they believed they had a real chance to win the presidency — but not with a black candidate. They felt Jackson would divide voters and the party, and thus lose in a national election.

The question on their lips, and one that would become *the* question of the entire 1988 campaign, was, "What does Jesse want?" Surely, they reasoned, he knows he can't become the nominee and president. He must be positioning himself, they guessed, for a major role in a Democratic administration, either as vice-president or a Cabinet member. Jesse's friend and adviser, Bert Lance, who had been budget director during the Carter Administration, found this line of reasoning amusing. A Cabinet position sounded interesting, Lance commented, but "if [Jesse's] already president, it may be hard for him to fill both jobs."

This kind of confidence was admirable. But as the primaries ground on, Jesse was finding his role as front-runner challenged. Michael Dukakis, governor of Massachusetts, was moving ahead of the other six remaining candidates, including Jesse. A moderately liberal Democrat who lacked Jesse's charisma and eloquence, Dukakis had a well-organized campaign and enough money behind him to go the distance.

Still, competition brought out the best in Jesse. He campaigned tirelessly in one state after another. He captured twenty percent of the votes in the Minnesota primary. Then came what the press called the "Michigan miracle." Just before the April primary, Dukakis was expected by many people to post an easy victory. After all, he had spent at least a million dollars in Michigan and had the solid endorsement of a number of local politicians, including Detroit's black mayor Coleman Young. But Jesse had worked hard to win the support of everyone from poor blacks and automobile workers to middle-class white liberals. The strategy succeeded better than even Jesse imagined it would. He won the Michigan primary with an astonishing fifty-five percent of the vote. It was the biggest win of any Democratic candidate outside of his home state.

Dukakis came in a distant second with twenty-nine percent of the vote. Far behind were Representa-

Jackson with, from left to right, former Governor of Arizona Bruce Babbitt, Senator Paul Simon of Illinois, Senator Albert Gore, Jr., of Tennessee, and Governor Michael Dukakis of Massachusetts prior to one of the debates held during the 1988 campaign for the Democratic nomination for President. Although Jackson ultimately lost his bid for the party's nomination, Jackson set an historical precedent for black people by attracting such widespread support.

tive Richard Gephardt, with thirteen percent, and senators Paul Simon and Albert Gore, each with two percent. Jackson explained his victory in simple terms: "It was the message, the authenticity and the soul of Jesse Jackson, versus the mechanics and the money of my opposition."

The effect of Michigan on the Jackson campaign was electric. He had become the superstar in an otherwise dull campaign season. The crowds doubled and tripled at every appearance Jesse made. Everyone wanted to shake his hand or get his autograph. His campaign contributions shot up to $60,000 a day. Before, his supporters chanted "Run, Jesse, Run!" at his appearances. Now they chanted "Win, Jesse, Win!" "There is a kind of Jackson-action fever in the air," the candidate happily observed. *Time* magazine, in its issue dated April 4, 1988, weighed in with this analysis: "[It] may take just one more major Jackson victory for the Democrats to seriously revise their calculation about whether a black preacher-politician who has never held public office can actually win the presidential nomination."

Winning was indeed a definite possibility. According to the latest delegate count, Jesse and Dukakis were running neck and neck. Dukakis had 653 delegates, and Jesse had 646. The only other candidate with substantial support was Albert Gore, with 381 delegates. A total of 2,082 delegates were needed to win the nomination.

The second week in April was disappointing for Jesse. Dukakis increased his lead by winning both the Wisconsin and Colorado primaries. Even so,

Jesse had nothing to be ashamed of in the Wisconsin race. In a state in which blacks made up only three percent of the population, he finished a respectable second, with twenty-eight percent of the vote. Paul Simon did so poorly, with five percent, that he decided to suspend his campaign. With Gephardt and Bruce Babbit of Arizona already out, that made it a three-man race from here on in.

Jesse's biggest and probably last hope to overtake Dukakis was less than a week away: the New York primary. New York's 255 delegates made it the second biggest prize of the campaign, after California, with its 363 delegates. Each of the three candidates desperately needed a victory in New York. Dukakis needed to win to maintain his lead into the home stretch. Jesse wanted to prove that he could repeat the "Michigan miracle." Gore had to win simply to stay in the race.

New York proved to be the toughest and most controversial primary to date. New York Mayor Ed Koch, a self-appointed spokesman for the city's large Jewish population, claimed that "Jews and other supporters of Israel have got to be crazy to vote for Jesse Jackson." This was a far cry from the same Ed Koch who some months earlier had said, "Jackson's fire, and the other candidates are like a cold shower." Gore, desperate to win in New York, unwisely accepted the Mayor's endorsement, and issued his own attack on Jackson's pro-Palestinian stand.

To make matters worse for Jesse, ugly rumors, completely unfounded, were spread that he had secretly kept his friendship with Black Muslim Louis

Farrakhan alive long after he had supposedly denounced Farrakhan and his anti-Jewish statements.
In reality, Jesse had worked hard to bind the wounds
between himself and the Jewish community. He had
hired several Jewish people on his staff, including his
campaign manager, Gerald Austin.

Jesse chose to stay away from the fray, to keep his
campaign positive and productive. He turned more
attention to the issue of drugs, a major concern of
most New Yorkers. He even made an effective antidrug television commercial, directed by young black
filmmaker Spike Lee. Jackson viewed the involve-
ment of his two rivals in the drug issue with some
amusement. "They're just sergeants and lieutenants
in the antidrug war," he pointed out. "I'm a five-star
general."

But the general didn't mount as effective a battle
strategy as he could have. The harsh criticism he was
getting on the Jewish issue made him gun-shy. In
other states, Jesse took his message directly to blue-
collar white neighborhoods and other groups. But in
New York, he spent most of his efforts in black and
Hispanic sections where he knew he would be welcomed. It may have been a fatal mistake.

Michael Dukakis won the New York primary hand-
ily, garnering fifty-one percent of the vote. Jesse came
in second, with thirty-seven percent, and Gore trailed
far behind again, with only ten percent. If Gore had
done better, it would have cut Dukakis's lead and
helped Jesse. As it was, the middle-of-the-road Dukakis benefited from the friction between the more conservative Gore and the more liberal Jackson.

With this loss, Jesse's dream of capturing the Democratic nomination was all but shattered. However, he was not bitter. He congratulated his rival and thanked him for running a clean campaign on the issues. On the other hand, unlike Gore, he was not yet ready to concede the nomination. Jesse realized that there were still millions of poor people, minority voters, and working-class whites who were counting on him to continue their fight. Jesse saw his job now as winning as many more delegates in the remaining primaries as possible. This would enable him to come to the Democratic convention in Atlanta with the power to influence the platform and issues the Democrats would run on in the fall election.

On a more personal level, he wanted something he had been fighting for all his life — respect and recognition. After two tries for the presidency, he felt he had earned respect for himself in the halls of political power. He had gone the distance in the long primary season and had gone further than any other candidate but Dukakis. And he had done all this as a black man with few resources other than his own charismatic personality, convictions, and dedication. Now he wanted to be allowed to "sit at the table" with the white politicians. He wanted to be in on the decision-making process that would affect all Americans. Whether he would obtain this respect was to be one of the main issues from now through the end of the Democratic campaign.

May brought no better news for Jesse. Dukakis beat him by almost a three-to-one margin in the Ohio and Indiana primaries. But although the "Duke," as he was now called, had beat his rival, he knew he would have to get along with him. Jesse Jackson had the largest group of supporters of any of his rivals. In fact, many of them felt stronger about Jesse than many of Dukakis's followers. The Massachusetts governor had to reach out to Jackson, to keep him and his supporters behind him in the fall campaign. On the other hand, he had to be careful not to give in too much to Jesse or risk losing support from moderate and conservative Democrats. It would prove to be a difficult balancing act.

As the convention loomed closer, the question of who Dukakis would select for his running mate became the main focus. Earlier, during a television debate, a reporter asked Jesse if he would be offered the vice-president slot on the ticket if he failed to be nominated. "I certainly will have earned serious consideration," he replied.

Dukakis gave serious consideration to Jesse and a number of other Democrats. While the vice-president has little power, it is still a position of influence. It is also a perfect platform for a person with ideas, energy, and ingenuity. Jesse Jackson was just that kind of man. But Dukakis felt he needed a running mate who would appeal to the moderates in the party and balance his own reputation as a liberal.

That man turned out to be Texas Senator Lloyd Bentsen. The Tuesday before the convention, Dukakis called the sixty-seven-year-old Bentsen at home and told him of his decision. Two hours later he called Jackson to let him know, but Jesse had left for the airport twenty minutes earlier and missed the call.

According to the Jackson staff, Dukakis had been told when Jesse was to leave and yet failed to call earlier. Later that day, arriving at his destination, Jackson was confronted by a reporter who asked him what he thought of Dukakis's choice for vice-president. Jesse was too surprised to speak. This was the first he had heard about it. A short time later at a press conference Jesse told reporters, "I'm too controlled, too mature to be angry." But the blow must have hurt. The respect he had struggled for still seemed to elude him. Much later, Dukakis's campaign manager called with an apology, but the damage had been done.

Two days after Dukakis's announcement, Jesse loaded up his friends and the press on six buses in Chicago and headed for Atlanta. Along the way they picked up delegates supporting Jesse. It was like one of the "freedom rides" of the civil-rights days, only now Jesse and his supporters were not going South as outsiders ready to protest. They were going as political insiders dedicated to changing the system legally.

Jackson and Dukakis both arrived at the convention on the weekend. While telling delegates at a reception that Jesse was wanted and needed, Dukakis stressed, "You can't have two quarterbacks. Every team has to have a quarterback. That's the nominee."

These were painful words for Jesse. They brought back unhappy memories of that white football coach at the University of Illinois. He too had told him there could only be one quarterback, and that that quarterback would always be white. Jesse assured his supporters that he would hold onto his delegates until a formal vote was taken on Wednesday night. "This is not a coronation," he said. "This is a convention. We're not talking about dictation, we're talking about democracy."

Would Jesse refuse to support Dukakis's candidacy? Would he disrupt the convention's nominating process? Would he leave the Democratic party and run for president as a third-party candidate? These questions were on the minds of a number of Democrats as the hours before the convention's opening ticked away.

At high noon on Monday, hours before the convention was to officially open, Dukakis and Jackson sat down with their campaign managers to iron out their differences. When the three-hour meeting was over, it seemed they had reached a new and productive understanding.

"I want Jesse Jackson to play a major role in the campaign," Dukakis said. "I want his supporters, who are out there by the millions, to be deeply involved in this campaign." But the word Dukakis used to describe their new relationship was "coalition," not "partnership." Jesse was to get a plane to carry him across the campaign trail in the fall. People in his campaign were to be given jobs in the national campaign. But little more was conceded. Democratic leaders were staunchly opposed to Jackson's efforts to make the party platform more liberal. In the eyes of many political observers, the platform was one of the shortest and dullest on record.

After his stunning speech on the second night of the convention, Jesse turned over center stage to his former rival. To no one's surprise, Dukakis was quickly nominated and confirmed as the presidential nominee. A few weeks later, the Republicans nominated George Bush, Ronald Reagan's vice-president, for president, and Senator Dan Quayle of Indiana for vice-president. The national campaign was at last underway.

At first, Jesse became in the words of *Time* magazine, "the invisible man of the campaign." The spotlight shifted to candidates Dukakis and Bush. Jesse withdrew from sight, sensitive to slights from the Dukakis team. But as the election drew closer, Jackson went on the campaign trail with a vengeance. He worked as hard as he had ever worked for his party and his candidate. On a typical day he would give a speech in New York in the morning, attend another event in Chicago by evening, and by the following day be speaking to a group of voters in Los Angeles. Jesse may not have seen eye to eye with Dukakis and his team, but he had no desire to see the Republicans in the White House for another four years. He still believed in the principles and the reforms of the Democratic party, and he would stand by them to the end.

The end, at least in 1988, came on Election Day in November. George Bush won an overwhelming victory. Dukakis and Bentsen carried only Massachusetts, the District of Columbia, and a few other states. However, while Bush won 426 electoral to Dukakis's 112, the popular vote was much closer. Bush won fifty-four percent, or 47,946,422 votes, while Dukakis won forty-six percent, or 41,016,429 votes.

As was true four years earlier, the defeat of his party was no defeat for Jesse Jackson. He emerged from the ashes of the election with his integrity and spirit intact. Despite all the ups and downs of the campaign trail, the shining victories and the dark disappointments, he had, in the end, earned the respect from the nation he had so dearly wanted.

This feeling was, perhaps, described best by two writers in *The New York Times* a month after the election. "No Presidential candidate of any party so eloquently and tirelessly described the needs of the nation and its citizens . . . " they wrote. "He was the dominant positive personality of the campaign. If he were not black, he would now be the president-elect."

11

The Endless Campaign

EARLY IN THE presidential campaign of 1988, Jesse Jackson explained to reporters that whether he won or lost, his life would continue as it had right along. "My future does not depend on one election," he said. "In a real sense, I'm running every day, every year."

If Jackson's life is an "endless campaign," as he himself has called it, the campaign continues. Since the 1988 election, he has remained an important figure on the political and social scene.

He has been active in campaigning for other candidates. After a successful first term as mayor in Chicago, Harold Washington was reelected in 1987. Tragically, only seven months into his second term, Washington died suddenly of a heart attack in his City Hall office. In a special election in 1989, Jackson supported another black candidate for mayor, Tim Evans. Denied the Democratic nomination, Evans ran on a third-party ticket. His main opponent was Richard M. Daley, who had lost to Washington in 1983. The voters were, predictably, divided along racial lines. But, interestingly, Daley was supported by several black leaders. One of them was Jesse's former convention manager, Ron Brown.

In February 1989, the forty-seven-year-old Brown was elected head of the National Democratic Committee. He is the first black to hold this prestigious position. Brown, with his middle-class background and experience as an urban lawyer, is a new kind of black leader. He is a bargainer, someone who believes in "give-and-take," whereas Jackson is more likely to confront people over the issues. In the mayoral election, Daley beat Evans in a campaign that renewed hostilities between Chicago's blacks and whites. The troubled city now needs both a Ron Brown and a Jesse Jackson to bring its people together again in peace and harmony.

No sooner was the Chicago election over than Jesse was turning his attention to another problem-ridden American city. This time, he was considering becoming a candidate himself.

In April 1989, Jesse told the press that he was thinking about running for mayor of the nation's capital, Washington, D.C., in November 1990. The news surprised the nation. But some of Jackson's closest friends and advisers had been urging him to run for mayor for weeks. Why?

For one thing, being mayor of Washington would give Jesse an opportunity to put his concerns and ideas into practice. Washington, with its high crime rate, serious drug problems, and soaring high school dropout rate, would engage all his talents and energies.

Secondly, being mayor would add an elective office to Jackson's résumé. This would also be additional proof that he was fully qualified to one day be president, if he should run again.

Finally, Jesse was said to see running for mayor as a way to help out an old friend in trouble. Three-term Washington mayor Marion S. Barry, Jr., a black, was being harshly criticized for his failure to stem the city's violent crime wave. He was also under investigation for his personal relationships with former associates accused of using and selling drugs. Jackson insisted he would never run against Barry. But his offer to run for mayor could give the mayor a graceful way out of his difficult situation. He would also be assured of leaving the mayor's office in capable hands.

With the election still months away, it is impossible to know what Jackson will do. If he does decide to run, he will undoubtedly become the front-runner. At the same time, he would face stiff competition from several local Democrats for the nomination. Two already-announced Democratic candidates, Sharon Pratt Dixon and City Councilman John Ray, have accused Jackson of being an outsider. They also said he would use the mayor's office as a stepping-stone to the presidency. However, if Jackson did become mayor, it would almost certainly put him out of the 1992 race for president. This possibility has relieved some Democrats. But it has troubled others, who wonder who would take Jesse's place as a candidate of the poor and needy.

A Jackson candidacy for mayor has stirred enthusiasm in the press and among the public. A few weeks after the story broke, *The New York Times* heartily approved, saying, "The man and the city could do wonders for each other. . . . Racked by drugs, crime, and all the afflictions of a large, dispirited underclass, Washington needs 'Jackson action'! . . . Governing Washington would require all Mr. Jackson's energy, imagination, and powers of persuasion. Doing it well would enhance his national stature and credibility. . . . "

While the public Jesse Jackson continues to take center stage in the national spotlight, the private man is a very different person. At home, away from the television cameras and the crowds, Jackson is quiet, serious, and thoughtful. In the family's large, rambling house on Chicago's South Side, he spends much of his time writing and listening to music. There is always a new speech to polish up and the regular deadline of his weekly newspaper column to be met. For relaxation he plays his favorite sport, basketball. There is a basketball hoop in the backyard, and in the early morning or after supper, Jesse enjoys a fast game or two with his two sons or adult co-workers and friends. His wife, Jackie, and his three daughters cheer them on from the lawn and keep score.

Jesse is extremely close to his five children. Jacqueline, Jr., better known as Jacky, is the only child living at home now. However, the Jackson clan gets together frequently on holidays, weekends, and during summer vacations. Christmas is their favorite holiday. Nearly every room in the house gets its own Christmas tree, and everyone pitches in in the kitchen, baking pies and cakes for the festive season.

Although his busy schedule keeps him on the road, Jackson tries to spend as much time at home as possible. When he can, he takes his children with him on trips around the nation and abroad. Jackie does her own traveling, often conducting "fact-finding missions" to help her husband. She also speaks and lectures frequently in Chicago and across the country.

Perhaps Santita, better known as Sandy, a medical student at Howard University, best sums up the way the Jackson children feel about their famous dad. "In addition to loving my father, I like him very much. He is a very open, warm person."

12

What Jesse Wants

WHEN PEOPLE TRY to understand this complex, fascinating man, they keep asking what he wants, as if the things that Jesse Jackson wants are different from what other people want. But, in fact, Jesse's desires are virtually the same as most Americans, and of people the world over. He wants to be a moral, responsible person, with his heart in the right place. He wants respect and recognition. He wants equality, justice, and economic freedom for the poor and the downtrodden. He wants an end to apartheid in South Africa, and peaceful solutions to other international problems and conflicts. He wants to be president, or maybe mayor of Washington, to help get the job done.

Jesse Jackson's incredible accomplishments serve as vivid evidence of personal strength and commitment to a goal. He overcame racism as a youth, worked hard to get an education, became a leader in the struggle for civil rights, and ran twice for president. In the process he has become a formidable politician and a progressive force for change in American society. His relentless drive and flair for the dramatic have given inspiration and hope to millions of Americans. Through captivating speeches and imaginative actions, he has done a remarkable job of publicizing his agenda and setting the course of political debate in the United States. Indeed, as one longtime Jackson staff person puts it, "You can't talk of the last twenty years without considering the 'Jesse factor.'"

Along the way he has been criticized for not "following through" on programs such as Operation Breadbasket, PUSH, and PUSH-Excel. While Operation Breadbasket worked well in Chicago, once Jackson turned it into a national operation it lost much of its effectiveness. PUSH was hugely successful in getting white businesses to promise to hire more blacks. However, some promises were quickly forgotten by the businesspeople who made them, and business went on as usual, often without further action taken by PUSH. PUSH-Excel's inspiration came mostly from Jesse's personal appearances at high schools. But once he left, many students found it difficult to achieve the scholastic goals he held up to them.

Jesse's response is: "I'm a tree shaker, not a jelly maker." In other words, he sees his role as someone who shakes things up, gets people thinking, and sets policy. He does not feel that he has to be the one to actually administrate those policies. In this regard, he can be compared to another "great communicator" — former President Ronald Reagan. Although the two men may have little else in common, they both have been extremely successful at capturing the nation's imagination.

After all the critics have spoken, Jesse Jackson remains an extraordinary figure on the American scene. His eloquence, compassion, and ability to lead and inspire are unparalleled. As a private citizen, preacher, and spokesperson for the underprivileged, he has had a greater effect on the political and social life of our country than most politicians of recent years. He has helped the helpless gain control over their economic and political futures by his work with PUSH and his countless voter-registration drives. He has given the hopeless a reason to hope. He has given the aimless a goal to strive for. He has fought against despair, drugs, war, weapons, and hatred. He has fought for love, peace, individual and ethnic pride and achievement. He has made a difference.

What of the next twenty years? At forty-seven, Jackson is still a relatively young man. Despite some health problems, such as his sickle-cell anemia, he is a powerhouse of energy who thrives on work. Whether he runs for mayor of Washington in 1990 or president again in 1992, it is difficult to imagine him retiring from the political arena in the foreseeable future. He will be there, as a political appointee, elected official, or private spokesperson.

One thing is certain. Whatever role Jesse Jackson takes on in the future, he will continue to be a model for those who need help and those of us who need to help. For Jesse Jackson, conscience of a nation, the campaign goes on.

Other books you might enjoy reading

1. Barker, Lucius J. *Our Time Has Come: A Delegate's Diary of Jesse Jackson's 1984 Presidential Campaign.* University of Illinois Press, 1988.

2. Chaplik, Dorothy. *Up With Hope: A Biography of Jesse Jackson.* Dillon, 1986. ·

3. Haskins, James. *The Life and Death of Martin Luther King, Jr.* Lothrop, Lee and Shepard, 1977.

4. Jackson, Jesse. *A Time to Speak: The Autobiography of the Reverend Jesse Jackson.* Simon and Schuster, 1988.

5. Kosof, Anna. *Jesse Jackson.* Franklin Watts, 1987.

6. Miller, Marilyn. *The Bridge at Selma.* Silver Burdett, 1985.

7. Witherspoon, William Roger. *Martin Luther King, Jr . . . To The Mountaintop.* Doubleday, 1985.

ABOUT THE AUTHOR

Steven Otfinoski has published many young adult novels, nonfiction books, and classroom plays. He is also the author of *Mikhail Gorbachev: The Soviet Innovator* in the Great Lives Series. He lives in Stratford, Connecticut with his wife and two children.